# Radical Initiatives in Interventionist and Community Drama

Edited by Peter Billingham



**intellect**™
Bristol, UK
Portland, OR, USA

First Published in the UK in 2005 by
Intellect Books, PO Box 862, Bristol BS99 1DE, UK.
First Published in the USA in 2005 by
Intellect Books, ISBS, 920 NE 58th Ave. Suite 300, Portland, Oregon 97213-3786, USA.


A catalogue record for this book is available from the British Library.

ISBN 1-84150-068-2
Cover Design: Gabriel Solomons
Copy Editor: Julie Strudwick
Production: May Yao

*Printed and bound in Great Britain by Antony Rowe Ltd.*

# Table of Contents

# Commissioning Editor's Introduction

From the moment when Robin Beecroft of Intellect Books, invited me to co-ordinate and commission a series of essays on contemporary examples of drama as intervention and community theatre, I was excited at the prospect. With excellent synchronicity, there were professional colleagues known to me, all of who were engaged or had recently been involved in a diverse and challenging range of work within this genre. Inevitably, the time, energy and process involved to bring these essays to published fruition has sometimes been daunting - both to contributors as well as myself. However, I believe that I can objectively, though not complacently, assert that the resulting collection of essays are of unmistakeable interest and significance to anyone involved in the analysis, recording or making of community theatre and interventionist drama strategies.

One of my initial criteria for commission, selection and inclusion was that the drama and theatre activities being recorded and evaluated should not have received previous published attention. This was in part to avoid the occasional disappointment of delving into anthologies of essays etc. on a theatre genre, only to discover an over regular, if perhaps inevitable, inclusion of specific author's and practitioner's texts. More importantly, I believed with conviction that the diverse ideological and methodological issues raised by the contributors' work were of considerable value to the wider debate concerning the nature and efficacy of drama-as-intervention within both the lives of individuals and communities.

I would like to take the opportunity to thank Professor John Bull for his articulate, informed and stimulating extended introduction to the essays, in which he provides a methodological and ideological context for the reader's understanding both these essays and also the meta-territory of drama as community and intervention. My own following summary of the essays in this volume is, I hope, a useful preliminary to Bull's more developed discussion and analysis:

Bill McDonnell's opening essay, 'Liberation theatre and the Nationalist struggle in Belfast 1984-90', is a detailed and passionate account and analysis of politicised community theatre, vibrant and challenging and yet - prior to McDonnell's research - largely unknown and unnoticed within British academic theatre debate. The significance that this hard-fought form of community theatre meant for the peoples of west Belfast as a form of both political identity and ideological struggle cannot be overestimated. Furthermore, the material conditions under which this theatre was made and documented, with all of the attendant British intelligence surveillance and censorship, is a necessary reminder of the continuing struggle for liberation and equality in Ireland. This is a struggle whose human cost has too often been camouflaged within the British media under the bleak euphemism of the soubriquet 'Troubles'. McDonnell is to be thanked by all who are interested or involved in the documentation and making of politicised community-located theatre.

In John Salway's exhaustive account of dissident community theatre in Sheffield, 'Bordering Utopia', he painstakingly re-creates the narratives and structures of making theatre in a contemporary English, urban context, whilst honestly identifying some of the issues and potential contradictions inherent within such projects. Salway is an immensely experienced community theatre worker and this experience and his continuing principled passion for politicised theatre is a defining quality of his account. As he identifies, in the postmodern context of the 'death of Socialism' (or at least, Soviet totalitarianism) arguing for a basis on which to launch, inspire and engage others within such enterprises can be viewed as problematic. Is the very act of seeking to make politicised theatre in the material conditions of early twenty-first century Britain 'utopian?' Not least are the definition, usage and demographic existence of 'community' and 'communities' as I reflected on in my own *Theatres of Conscience*:

> Community, of course, has become a much used and misused contemporary term in both politics and the arts. Its employment within a reactionary, Thatcherite vocabulary, for example, 'Care in the Community', has become synonymous with a political culture similar to that envisioned in Orwell's 1984. In other words, language is used to conceal, invert and rationalise the self-interest of realpolitik strategies...This Thatcherite model incorporates an inescapably reactionary notion of a 'community-culture' defined by individual self-help and self-reliance...It must also be said that in its resurrected use in liberal contexts such as Community Arts, its implicit meaning can come perilously close to an uncritical, even nostalgic idealisation of working-class or ethnic communities.(Billingham, 2002, p.91)

On this point, Velda Harris' lucid and intellectually rigorous account of her project with students taking drama to marginalized tribe-communities in Azerbaijan, raises important issues about some of the uncritical assumptions present within the debate and practice surrounding multi and inter-culturalist art forms. Critically aware of the related function and metaphor of the *dues ex machina* of classical theatre, Harris interrogates with admirable clarity and intellectual honesty, the ideological implications of simply 'parachuting in' upon other peoples, languages, traditions and eco-economies: the very material conditions of their lives. From what viewing-position does the theatre worker locate her/his engagement, participation and intervention? Her discussion and analysis are a timely and singular reminder, I believe, to all practitioners, researchers and commentators engaged in multi-cultural and cross-cultural activities and debates. Our own political culture and ideological climate (conveying the Blairite denial of 'ideology') has shown us all too easily how peoples of other races and ethnicities can be swiftly - almost simultaneously - exoticised or demonised.

Carole Christensen's clear and uncluttered discussion of her work with immigrant, asylum-seeking and often traumatised women in Copenhagen offers the reader a focused and provisionally optimistic insight into how drama can facilitate self-confidence, cultural and social integration - perhaps even incorporating a small measure of helpful psychological readjustment. Christensen has worked for many years now as a teacher and theatre worker in Denmark and Sweden and her compassionate but unsentimental approach is a commendable role model for those engaging in similar kinds of therapeutic role-play work. It is very much to be hoped that the recent election of a right-wing government in 2002 does not pre-empt the withdrawal of State funding and support for this kind of invaluable work.

Finally, the essay by hugely experienced theatre director and actor trainer, Gunduz Kalic, captures all of the verve, immediacy and sheer practicality of his radicalised community theatre in Australia. Kalic has remained unswervingly committed to the social, ideological and interventionist role of theatre through a life that has included working with Joan Littlewood and helping to found (and be an early Director of) East 15 Theatre School. Celebrating the anarchic and transformational quality and potential within 'theatre as play' Gunduz Kalic embodies a popular, politicised radicalism characterised by unflinching integrity and humour - uncompromising to all narrow, prescriptive hegemonies.

I would like to express my sincere thanks to all of the contributors and to the various individuals and communities that they have worked in, for and through. I also wish to thank Robin Beecroft for having the faith to commission this book from me and to Masoud Yazdani, May Yao and everyone else at Intellect that have helped to make the production of this book possible. Equally and unequivocally, I want to extend my thanks to Sally Ashworth for her final proofreading of the manuscript and her careful and methodical compilation of the index. Last, but not least, I would like to thank my colleagues at Bath Spa University College, especially Dr Geoff Smith, Dr Tim Middleton and Professor Paul Edwards for supporting the final stages of the editing of these essays through the provision and support of a reduced teaching load at a significant stage in the preparation of this manuscript.

On a personal note, many thanks, as always, to my partner Marilyn for her good humour and unyielding belief in the project.

Peter Billingham

## Reference

Peter Billingham, *Theatres of Conscience 1939-53, a study of four touring British Community Theatres*, (Routledge Harwood), 2002.

# Introduction: On Interventionist and Community Theatre

The five essays in this collection present a series of descriptive and analytical accounts drawn from first-hand experience of a variety of community theatre schemes in Britain and abroad. Individually, these essays offer exciting accounts of individual projects; but, apart from emphasising the continuing strength of the 'movement', collectively they also offer some very different senses of what might be understood as community theatre. Thus, the collection will be valuable both as a series of templates well worthy in any consideration of the creation of community theatre, and as a basis for discussion about the chimerical nature of the activity.

Bill McDonnell's 'A Good Night Out on the Falls Road: Liberation theatre and the Nationalist struggle in Belfast 1984-1990' borrows John McGrath's title from his published Cambridge lectures on the politics of popular theatre (John McGrath, 1981); and it does so in order to claim an affinity with the kind of political theatre there promulgated by McGrath. That is to say, that it should be popular, entertaining and instructive. But, if it does borrow from McGrath's title, it does so with a certain sense of grim irony, for the description of the performance that forms the centre of this essay is of something that is more harrowing than entertaining. This is because, although there may be a paralleling of intent, the projects described by McDonnell differ from McGrath's work with 7:84, in that they come from within a defined community rather than being brought in by an external theatrical company, and the experiences drawn upon to produce the work are immediate and extremely frightening.

McDonnell provides useful contextualisation for the works, tracing the development of the 'Troubles' in Ireland from the late 1960s on, before considering the nature of liberation theatre. He then looks at the work of the Belfast Community Theatre and Belfast People's Theatre. The most graphic section is an account of a performance of *Sign on the Dotted Line* at Conway Mill on the Falls Road in March 1987:

> The theatre is created in a cell, a kitchen, a community space, a theatre and in one man's head. It arrives through the agency of cigarette papers smuggled in mouths from a prison, a tape recorder, paper and pen, debate and argument. It is begun by men, and taken forward with a deeper agenda by women. It is part reportage, part text, and part improvisation. A particular issue, interrogation, becomes a prism through which other experiences are refracted. However, while the script exists, and can be re-interpreted, what cannot be reproduced in this process is the collective 'method' by which this play came to be made. It was a method conjured out of the

interaction of people with an unstable reality, and negotiated amid politically created limitations on access, resources, space and time.

McDonnell's account of the performance, delivered in the present tense, does, however, give a very vivid and disturbing enactment of the event and the circumstances of its creation and performance.

The rest of the projects are written not, as this is, from the point of view of a sympathetic observer, but from that of the instigators of the projects. John Salway's 'Bordering Utopia: Dissident community theatre in Sheffield' describes the activities of Sheffield Popular Arts from 1998-2000 in putting together a community performance that would offer a rather different approach to the millennium celebrations than would come via the government, local councils and the like. It is a painstaking blow-by-blow account (sometimes almost literally) of the process from inception, through rehearsal to performance, and the essay is concluded with reflections on the efficacy of community theatre:

> Its greatest strength remains, of course, the fact that it is the art form that is the closest to the textures of actual social life. Although capable of exploiting the potential of complex technologies, in essence it requires simply the presence of human beings together in a shared time and space. To make it requires only the ability to move and speak. It is truly accessible to everybody, if only they can overcome the barriers that stop them believing in themselves.

The essay's particular honesty comes from the reiterated awareness that the instigators of the project might have a slightly different agenda to that of the community participants: it is a dilemma central to the development of all such projects, and its articulation, both as a theoretical and a practical issue, adds much weight to the account.

In contrast, the other three essays describe projects that, in very different ways, take on an international dimension. Carole Angela Christensen's 'Crossing Boundaries and Struggling for Language: Using drama with women as a means of addressing psycho-social-cultural issues in a multi-cultural context in contemporary Copenhagen' describes what is, superficially at least, a more directly educational enterprise - the use of drama as a tool to assist 'immigrant and refugee women suffering from psychological trauma and stress symptoms, where learning ability is inhibited'. What the account of the progress of the seventeen women involved in the project demonstrates succinctly is that the development of the language and communications skills necessary for their adjustment to life in a new country cannot be separated from the reasons why they were there anyway. Christensen acknowledges the work of both Boal and Howard Gardner in her approach to the task, writing of the latter that:

> [he] proposes that genuine acquisition of knowledge is a process where not only factual knowledge is acquired, but also one where understanding takes place. In this important respect, drama conventions provide opportunities for different aspects of

life to be explored in a fictionalised context. Through this process, participants have the opportunity to take on other identities within that fictionalised context, facilitating not only a deeper understanding of the corresponding actual situation, but also encouraging a more free and fluent use of the new language.

It is a particular strength of the essay that Christensen is able to argue for the wider scope of the project, even as she questions its efficacy in the end product.

Velda Harris's 'Parachuting In: Issues arising from drama as intervention within communities in Azerbaijan' describes a project arising from a T.I.E. course that transported British students to work in refugee camps in Azerbaijan. The enterprise had begun with a Central School of Speech and Drama initiative, working with an inner city London school with a group of Additional Language (EAL) students, including a number of Bosnian refugees. Paralleling this, two Central students had spent time in Azerbaijan the previous year working on an Arts Residency project. Harris describes the bringing together of these various strands of an educational programme, the decision to work towards taking the T.I.E. students to the camps, and what ensued thereafter. She prefaces the account with a thorough theoretical survey of the problems inherent in such an operation, insistent that there must be some way of bridging the very different experiences of the two communities, which she labels as 'source' and 'target':

> For the adults in the Azeri camps the memories of home and sense of loss is still very keen. There is very little hope that they will return to their homeland and very few have been relocated or found employment beyond the camp or its immediate locality... For most of the men there was little to do except try to scratch a living from the stony ground, provide an occasional taxi service for visitors, but more usually play dominos and smoke for recreation. The women were busier, engaged in domestic tasks, hand washing the family's clothes, and cooking on primitive stoves in cramped conditions or out of doors. For the children there was school for half a day, and little to occupy them for the rest of the time. Any break in this monotonous routine, like the arrival of a food shipment, or visits by aid workers, brought out a crowd of men eager to observe or participate in the action. Many of the children could remember no other life, but their memories of their homeland were sustained by the stories told by their parents.

And it was through the use of dramatised stories that the attempt to inter-connect was made. Harris concludes: 'A pebble has been dropped into a pool. We hope the ripples will continue to spread'.

The project described by Gunduz Kalic is again very different. His title, 'Taking Liberties', refers to the name of the Australian Theatre Group of which he was Artistic Director in the 1990s. It is a title that invokes both the notion of people seizing liberty, and essentially medieval ideas of Jesters and Lords of Misrule, as well as Bakhtin's concept of carnival. The company's credo was well summarised by its entry in an Australian performing arts yearbook: 'Taking Liberties Theatre Company, Australia's Court Jester... poignantly mad, seriously funny, joyfully biting political theatre... see a Fool, break a rule, take a liberty', as well as by its sub-heading, 'A Foolish Theatre Company' on posters. It sought to take theatre to non-conventional venues and to audiences who would not normally go to the theatre. In essence it offered a version of exactly the kind of strategy advocated by John McGrath in the title of the book invoked by Bill McDonnell in the first essay in the collection.

This short account of the five projects should already give some sense of the different models of community theatre adopted, and the degree of shared and divergent strategies. It should stress, in particular, the extent to which the notion of community theatre is both eclectic in its sourcing and by no means homogenous in its practice. For, viewed either historically or generically the term 'Community Theatre' can be interpreted in a number of different ways: the problem being that these different takes on the term are not always mutually exclusive but may, nonetheless, often be quite hostile one to the other. Theatrical practice can come from, and exist with, for and on behalf of the community, the last relationship including the possibility of an educative or propagandist element. The only relationship that cannot be nurtured or sustained is one of outright antagonism to the community, in the same way that no mainstream theatre can afford consciously to put on a production - *Springtime for Hitler* excepted - that will deliberately alienate its potential audience to the extent that it will vote with its feet and either not come to the performance or make a noisy exit.

That said, however, it is not always as simple as this, for the formulation assumes that any given community audience has an ideologically uniform composition, and this is never really the case. A presentation of a piece that calls into question patriarchal attitudes, for instance, may divide an audience, however theoretically enlightened, in a potentially very complicated way, based on differences of gender, age, and so on. Highland and island audiences for the 7:84 tour of John McGrath's *The Cheviot, the Stag and the Black Oil* would not have consisted entirely of descendants of people who had been dispossessed of their land in the clearances: there will have been also members of the audience who had benefited from them. Although the general point holds, then, it does suggest a need to be very wary in making assumptions about community constituency. One particularly startling example of the importance of identifying the specific nature of the audience is evidenced in Gunduz Kalic's essay on the activities of the Australian Foolery group, Taking Liberties. A satirical piece about the workings of the then Australian government, it could accurately be described as a piece of community theatre for the majority of its performances. However, when the company, which included Kalic, conned their way into giving a performance of a production extremely critical of the Australian Government in Parliament House itself, the changed nature of the audience meant that what had previously been a piece of community theatre was now more obviously guerrilla theatre. In the spirit of the change, there was no suggestion of an invitation to give a repeat performance.

The variety of potential relationships, relationships that are rarely mutually exclusive, means that 'Community Theatre' is in danger of becoming an all-purpose portmanteau concept, of little use save as a label of political convenience. Below I give a list of different concepts of community theatre. The intention is not to offer a comprehensive catalogue, but rather to use the list as a basis for considering the problems that arise in attempting any kind of categorisation.

## Community Theatre Models: An indicative list

• **Amateur Community Theatre Groups.** Motivation: to participate in dramatic production; and social. Usual venues: (a) own 'theatre'; (b) hired premises (Church Halls, University Theatres, etc.); (c) local professional theatres (an important part of the economy of the receiving theatre, in that there are no production costs involved, and there will be at the very least a cut of the box office, plus bar receipts, etc.). Audience: a community one, in the sense that a lot of it will be formed from family and friends of the participants and, especially if using own premises or a regular venue, will have built up a following of supporters. Plays produced: could be anything, but usually with a leaning towards the mainstream and popular - comedies, thrillers, musicals, etc. Self-supporting.

• **Youth Theatre Groups.** Often, but by no means always, based on professional theatres and arts venues. The prime motivation is the building up of theatrical skills within a local youth community, but it will also frequently involve the conscious exploration of themes particularly relevant to that community. Usually, but not always, fund-supported.

• **Community Theatre in the Professional Theatre.** This may include the frequent encouragement of local writing (the use of Willy Russell at the Liverpool Everyman, for example), involve a more consistent policy of aiming productions at a local community (such as Peter Cheeseman's work in Stoke-on-Trent, Alan Ayckbourn's work in Scarborough, and particularly the early work of John Godber for Hull Truck), or may be quite sporadic (the revivals of *The Stirrings in Sheffield on a Saturday Night* at Sheffield's Crucible Theatre, for example). It would also include the programme of 'Tribune' plays produced at the Tricycle Theatre in Kilburn, London, where the work is produced for a community that may be thought of as politically as well as geographically located. It is usually community theatre in the sense that it is aimed at a local community or at targeted sections of a local community. However, as with the ongoing efforts of Philip Hedley at the Theatre Royal, Stratford East over more than a twenty year period, this may also include the active encouragement of local participation, in this instance with the continuing policy of producing work by new Black and Asian groups drawn from the local community, as with its current production, *The Black Life*, a musical about Black Britons today. Touring productions, either from a home-based theatre or from freestanding companies may also come into this category. Usually fund-supported but, interestingly, in the case of the Theatre Royal Stratford East the theatre's bid for Arts Council support to help research and create Black Musical Theatre was turned down.

• **Theatre-in-Education.** This may involve the importation of professional (perhaps theatre-based, probably financially supported) companies into schools, colleges and (less frequently) institutions of Higher Education, bringing productions that centre on particular issues (racial equality, bullying, etc.). Frequently there will be a strong participatory element involving the targeted audience. Thus, often it is better to think of such efforts as ongoing projects rather than, necessarily, one-off performances. The aim is then, in part, to create a sense of community between the performers and the spectators. Very often the advertised ground, the primary aim, of the project may not be the sole area of dialogue: as Carole Angela Christensen describes in her paper on a Danish project on language acquisition for women immigrants, 'the secondary *Invisible* goal... was far more venturesome... giving the clients the opportunity to create dramatisations of significant or traumatic moments in their lives,' hoping thus that 'the individuals would gain the motivation and means to cope with life demands and function more creatively within their new country and culture'. Usually funded or even specifically commissioned.

• **Educational Community Group.** Activity: courses incorporating community theatre practice. Following on from the above, productions may also arise from course-work done at such institutions at, in particular, HND, BA or MA level, where the intention is to reach targeted community audiences outside the institutions. An example of is to be found in this collection in Velda Harris' paper. Again, as above, there may be other than the stated primary aim. Funded.

• **Special Interest Theatre Companies.** This would include Reminiscence and, on occasions, Heritage Theatre, theatre for the deaf, the blind, etc. It is sometimes a theatre that is site-specific, but usually takes productions/projects to host institutions. It may simply offer a take on a given area but, most often, involves directly working with, for example, deaf or blind people. Usually funded, often with specific commissions.

• **Theatre in the Workplace.** Professional theatre companies working to commissions to produce work (frequently interactive) dealing with specific issues relating to the activities of the institutions or organisations booking them.

• **One-Off Community Celebrations, Festivals, Pageants, etc.** May be straightforward local celebrations connected with a national (the Queen's Jubilee, for example) or a local event (such as the centenary of a charter), and will normally not have any overt political aim (though it will, perforce, at the very least represent the dominant ideological interests). Thus, it usually sets out to be quite all embracing, with something for everyone. Self-supporting.

• **Theatre from Within the Community.** Theatre that is entirely created by and for a definable community. The lines of demarcation between this and the final category are not always easy to draw: the Sheffield project described in this collection, for example, in one sense falls into this slot, but it does contain a clear sense of leadership/initiation from individuals who cannot automatically be thought of as being directly from the community in a very specific sense. Equally,

Ann Jellicoe's regular community productions did draw from the inner community resources but made use of imported playwrights (Jellicoe, 1987). The Belfast projects outlined by Bill McDonnell are a good example of the kind. Self-supporting.

• **Theatre For the Community.** Related strongly to the above but created by companies on tour or in residence. This may be a kind of Commune Theatre work: permanent theatre companies working in and with a designated community: frequently concerned with ecological and environmental issues, with a desire to link them to larger issues, in particular late capitalism and globalisation: the best-known example is Welfare State International. It may involve community-based companies working on localised one-off issues (a rent strike, for example), or touring theatre aimed at particular non-localised constituencies, for instance feminist theatre. The companies may be professional or not: in the former case, often funded.

It is a somewhat strange list, yoking together not only activities that are patently quite disparate but also those that are ideologically opposed. In several instances, words other than 'community' might seem more appropriate: constituency, for instance, or the word that Carole Angela Christensen uses to describe her 'audience' in her essay, 'clients', where the emphasis is given to a service being provided for an agreed transfer of money. This might seem particularly relevant to the 'Theatre in the Workplace' category; but if we consider, say, an organisation being offered an interactive performance/project on equal opportunities or disability, it is clear that there is a sense of 'community' at work for both the providers and the hosts. There may, therefore, also be the possibility of conflict, of interests, of ideology, and so on, between providers and hosts. But a consideration of the very notion of 'community' must be the starting point.

At base these problems arise because, like so many social and cultural descriptors, the notion of 'community' is not neutral. Its usage has been associated with a sharing of common interests (from its Latin root, *communitatem*), and also a sharing of common location (Williams, 1976, pp. 65-66). Thus, it can be taken to imply, in its largest common denominational sense, little more than a group of people who happen to be living in one particular designatable area as opposed to another; and at the other extreme, a closely knit constituency, perhaps (but not necessarily) defined in terms of a common geographical location, with a sense of a common and unifying group ideology (be it politically or class based), defined by questions of sexuality or gender, by racial origin or religious beliefs, or whatever.

In the pre-industrial world, before the real process of urbanisation had begun - when even London was still essentially a series of villages surrounded by open land - community could be seen in terms of village/hamlet culture; and a great deal of what still describes itself as community theatre can be seen as relating to this sense (One-off Community Celebrations, Festivals, Pageants, etc. list above) - historical pageants celebrating the past of a particular settlement, for example. However, even such events as these are not value-free, as Alan Ayckbourn explored in his theatrical account of one such small town undertaking, in *Ten Times Table* (1977). Plans for the re-enactment of an agricultural protest in the town are increasingly threatened by the members of the organising committee dividing on class lines, one half taking the bosses' side and the other the workers'.

RAY: The story of the Pendon Twelve... Following the increasing rise of discontent amongst agricultural folk brought about by these new taxation laws, two local men, Jonathan Cockle and William Brunt, began actively to ferment this feeling through a series of meetings when, according to one contemporary witness, Cockle 'spoke with much fire and feeling' whilst Brunt 'would further inflame the crowd with his fierce appearance and wild behaviour'...

HELEN: Does it go on much longer about these awful looking men?

ERIC: I shouldn't imagine they had a great deal of option as to how they looked... They were men, may I remind you, who spent their working lives sweating their guts out for a living.

HELEN: My dear boy, there are people round this table who, as you charmingly put it, sweat their guts out for a living. I do for one, but I don't go round covered in black hair throwing people in the air for fun.

ERIC: They were probably living at starvation level to start with...

HELEN: No, the trouble with them was they spent all their time making speeches. Getting drunk. Throwing people in the air. Serve them jolly well right. (Ayckbourn, 1982, pp. 80-81)

And inexorably the pageant descends into farcical chaos, as both sides plot to use the event as a means of declaring their political position. What is revealed through this fictitious attempt at a community project is the lack of a unified community. But what Ayckbourn presents comically is always a serious issue in such undertakings, and not just in the kind of broad-stroke project outlined in this play. Even in a more integrated project, differences may easily surface, as John Salway describes in 'Bordering Utopia', where we learn that several members of the team 'left because they were not happy with the political beliefs that underpinned what we were doing'. As Bill McDonnell stresses in the first part of his essay in this collection, history is always a contested site. Furthermore, versions of Ayckbourn's ideological dispute may frequently prove central to such a project, when two different notions of community clash: that of the simple fact of living within a particular area set against an adherence to a particular set of values that may not, in fact, be 'common'. Baz Kershaw gives a telling example of this in relation to Welfare State's *Town Hall Tattoo* in Barrow, a 'celebration' of the centenary of Queen Victoria's Jubilee Year. It was, he says, 'extraordinary for its integration of acceptable civic celebration, extravagantly anarchic imagery, and a subtle radicalism which poked gentle fun at the very values the event appeared to valorise'. (Kershaw, 1992)

This tension relates exactly to the way in which the term 'community' has developed. As Williams argues, from the nineteenth century 'the sense of immediacy or locality was strongly developed in the context of larger and more complex industrial societies' and the word began also to be used to describe 'experiments in an alternative kind of group living' (Williams, 1976, pp. 65-66). This precisely describes the actual/potential ideological clash in the Welfare State project. The reason for this is clearly that the notion of community has continued to retain its sense of smaller unit (smaller, that is, than the nation or the town), and has become associated with ideological constructions that oppose in one way or another (a religious community or a village of striking miners, to take two very different examples) the predominant and assumed-to-be hegemonic values of the larger society.

All of the essays in this collection are concerned with what can be described as interventionist community theatre: that is to say, a theatre that seeks to directly affect the lives of its targeted audiences. The sense of community associated with the specifics of locality is central to many such projects (that is to say, the ones where the notion of 'client' is least applicable), and very frequently it operates to offer an alternative vision of how things were or might be in the future. The use of the past, usually a pre-capitalist past, as in the evocation of the seventeenth century diggers in the Sheffield project, is often allied with a specifically non-urban context.

> In the discussion that followed, participants spoke about changes in our conception of what a 'community' is. The idea of a shared geographical area or locality still strongly suggests itself. But the development of urban lifestyles has meant the break-up of simple face-to-face relationships in neighbourhoods: people seek their social identity and solidarity more and more in communications across distances. 'Communities' can be exiled peoples who maintain contact across the globe; or people who share a particular political or religious commitment or leisure pursuit. Where there are face-to-face relations, questions of relative freedoms and responsibilities are easier to reconcile: it becomes more difficult with the real social fragmentation that comes with the growth of cities and the destruction of traditional communities rooted in the soil.

In more conservative community theatre practice, this recall of a rural past can easily be linked to a version of pastoral nostalgia, a rose-tinted 'folk-memory' of an historical period when life was supposedly much simpler, when all the people pulled together, and so on. That it should be evoked so often in a questioning theatre not enshrined with the values of the status quo gives evidence of the residual strength of the concept: for rural history can be visited for evidence of dissidence - the concept conjured within John Salway's essay on Sheffield - as well as for settled complacency.

Interestingly, talking about what he describes as 'Radical Theatre' Baz Kershaw writes that what is 'under scrutiny here is the British alternative theatre movement, and the "form" that is the focus of this book's individual studies is community-oriented theatre, in the shape of key practices undertaken mostly in *rural* areas'. (Kershaw, 1992, p. 5: my emphasis) That he is able to argue thus results largely from his choice of companies, but it also bears witness to the significance of such companies in the development of a British community theatre movement. In what is probably the most famous community theatre production, McGrath's *The Cheviot, the Stag and the Black Oil*, the rural past operates as a contested site for both the location and the subject of most of the play's narrative, and furthermore it was played on the very sites of that contestation, with the text being revised from performance as the tour developed in order to introduce directly local references to that past struggle.

However, to make such a decision about the work of the companies to be discussed means that the great amount of specifically city-based work is largely unconsidered and, as it happens, it is varieties of this that concern the majority of writers in this collection. The Sheffield project was certainly embarked on with a strong sense of the specifically rural roots of the notion of community, as is evident in the passage quoted above, but there is absolutely no echo of this in the community theatre practice in Belfast analysed by Bill McDonnell. The reasons are not hard to discern.

The Belfast community groups that he writes about are not the products of intervention from outside: they were produced directly by and for the community within which both theatre workers and audience live. The enclosed nature of the activity (necessarily enclosed because of the nature of the plays, and the threat that they represented to the authorities) means that such projects go largely unreported - not just because even local newspapers carry no account of them, but because the synchronicity of text, performers and audience acts as an excluding mechanism, rendering them effectively invisible to an outside world. After the Miners' Strike of 1984-5, many productions by writers sympathetic to the cause were available to a larger public - usually because they had been performed in conventional theatrical spaces - but we look in vain for any account of the many productions that were put together by and for the mining communities themselves.

This sense of community cohesion between performers and audience introduces a further point about community theatre. In most writing about performance, debate about the exact nature of the relationship between performance and audience occurs, but there is an over-riding assumption that the actors have something to offer and the audience something to receive, passively or not. Not all participants in community theatre today would necessarily accept such a model being ascribed to their activities, however. In John Salway's account of Dissident Community Theatre in Sheffield (quoted above), a project with very particular political aims, the writer concludes that the actual performance of the improvised play was not really the ultimate goal of the exercise: 'In the practice of community theatre, it is the journey itself which is the destination', the stress here being laid on the educative role of the project for the participants, rather than the audience. Bill

McDonnell, in his account of the work of the Belfast Community Theatre, also lays emphasis on the multiplicity of motivations on the part of participants: 'There were those who, like Reid [Joe Reid, activist and founder member of the group] saw it as a political vehicle, a means of conscientization and mobilisation: for others it offered the simple opportunity to act: for others still it was a refuge, a source of comradeship, care and support'. Inevitably, these different motivations may result in clashes or withdrawal, as in the Sheffield project. For many, the chief and declared point of such activities is quite simply an 'involvement in developing a theatre which breaks down cultural barriers and encourages people to make their own plays'. That is to say, that the activity is concerned not so much with the defining of a community ethos as with the creation of it; not so much with the desire to tell a particular story or develop a particular thesis as with the liberation of the individual imagination in 'play'. The quotation immediately above comes from the back cover of a fascinating collection of essays about community theatre over a nearly forty year period in one English city, *People Make Plays: Aspects of Community Theatre in Hull Since 1955* (Pamela Dellar, 1992). What makes it particularly fascinating is that the editor has been at pains not to present any single view of what might constitute or have constituted community theatre in Hull during this period. Projects in which the prime desire has evidently simply been to make theatre sit alongside the work of the University of Hull's Drama Department, 'theatre for children, for the disabled, for the cause of feminism, for special community work, for experimental projects, and so on'. (Hoggart, 1992, p. vii) Community here is seen to have a double sense: firstly of the more local and specialised, and secondly in its collectivity, as constituting evidence of Hull itself as a vigorous community.

The notion of community becomes far more extended however, when activity takes on a truly international dimension. The two most obvious examples of this in the essays in this collection are Carole Angela Christensen's account of a Danish project on language acquisition for women immigrants, and Velda Harris' essay on the 'issues arising from the adaptation of British models of drama and Theatre in Education, first in work devised for refugee children in a London school; and secondly, during short visits over a three year period, in work with young people in displaced persons' camps in Azerbaijan'. At the start of her essay, Velda Harris uses Conceison to ask a question that haunts every one of the case studies in this collection: 'We must ask ourselves not only what we are doing, but also how we are doing it. Are such projects actually fostering understanding and cultural sharing or are they merely reifying hegemonic structures and painful misconceptions?' Her piece is aptly entitled 'Parachuting In: Issues arising from drama as intervention within communities in Azerbaijan'. The two key phrases are 'parachuting in', with its deliberate sense of an aerial swoop being made, and 'drama as intervention', where there is an honestly self-conscious statement of intent. It raises issues that are central to virtually all the essays in the collection.

Any attempt to consider the nature and function of community theatre is immediately beset by the problematics of interculturalism. This will be the case in any kind of interventionist theatre, as we have seen with the earlier example of the

Welfare State project, drawn from Kershaw. In the case of the Belfast theatre projects described by McDonnell the problem does not arise because audience, performers and writers share a common social and ideological base - the only divide being between the imprisoned writers smuggling out their texts bit by bit on cigarette papers and the recipients and animators of the text in the outside community. However, as soon as there is any kind of separation of experience between 'incoming' practitioners and a 'host' audience, interculturalist problematics perforce enter the equation. At the very least this may be concerned with coming at the audience from a more culturally or politically privileged position, risking patronising the very people intended to be entertained and informed; at the worst it may involve effectively stealing the cultural models of the receiving community in order to convert/subvert them into what is seen as a more appropriate ideological model. But it is obviously a much larger concern the further apart the incoming and the host communities are in a cultural sense, where vast geographical distances and different languages, experiences and political and cultural models are in juxtaposition. Harris sums up the problems succinctly:

> The issue of perspective is of fundamental importance in the consideration of theatre in an intercultural context... It has become common currency in discussion of intercultural theatre practice to distinguish between a source culture from which a particular theatrical performance is derived and a target culture in which the 'translated' performance is presented to an audience... It is a cultural and artistic model from a British source that will undergo the process of adaptation. This will be determined by the 'perspective of the adapters' (the students involved in the project) whose choice of form will be informed by their research into the artistic, social and cultural models provided by the target culture. In deciding on an appropriate holding form they will need to consider what 'reception adapters' they can build into the work and the readability of the performance. The complexities involved in 'translating' a performance from a source to a target culture are further complicated in this case by the fact that the 'perspective of the adapters' includes an educational methodology, and by the particular experience and needs of the target audience.

As she writes later, 'In any kind of intercultural encounter the participants carry with them the accumulated baggage of history and its scarcely recognised manifestations in contemporary attitudes and behaviour'. In his *Theatre and the World*, Bharucha embarked on a full-scale onslaught on what he constructed as, effectively, an intercultural project that can be traced from the writings of Craig and Artaud to that of Grotowski and (his particular 'villain') Richard Schechner. That he should have reserved his most venomous treatment for Schechner is not that surprising, given that he more than anyone has been responsible for the attempt to create a general Performance Theory that, in its essential insistence on an 'anthropological' approach, privileges commonality over difference, connection over 'otherness'.

> For all its play and ambivalence, this theory upholds a methodology and a vision of the world that must be termed ethnocentric. Apart from decontextualising 'ritual actions' from their larger structures (and thereby neutralising their meanings),

> Schechner seems more eager to synthesis underlying patterns of structure/process in differing performance traditions rather than to confront their individual histories. This eclecticism is almost as problematic as his advocacy of 'cultural tourism', which tends to be examined on a purely technical level as a generator of new performances, rather than as an instance of the cultural exploitation of non-Western people. (Bharucha, 1993, p. 3)

Now, of course, Bharucha is not writing about community theatre as such, but rather about the process by which, in particular, Western culture embarks on Indiana Jones style 'raids' on what may effectively be described as varieties of community theatre in non-western indigenous cultures. I use the term 'community theatres' here - in the realisation that it is a slightly unusual appropriation of the term - in the sense that it is the shared values of the given community that Bhrarucha feels to be directly under a double threat; that of being somehow 'contaminated' by external cultural influences, and of being looted as surely as is evidenced by the amassed artefacts in the British Museum and elsewhere from earlier, more material raids.

Harris conjures with the division between the anthropological, universalising and the local, particularising models in her essay and that, in essence, she attempts to have it both ways is not that surprising. There is evidently a case to be argued for the particular in relation to locating the separable issues that concern one 'community' as against another; but those separable issues are not ever really that separable. A piece of community theatre that seeks to involve itself in the protest against a new motorway being built on old forest land, for example, cannot in practice remain solely within the local community domain if it is to have any real purchase on the wider issues: questions of public and private transport usage, of ecology, and so on. It does not take much effort to extend an argument about the fight over a small parcel of land in Britain to one about the worsening condition of the Brazilian rainforests. Worries about interculturalism in neo-imperialist terms have come to seem increasingly pertinent not because, in Marshall McCluhan's famous phrase of the 1960s, the world is becoming a 'global village' (a phrase that plays with a kind of notion of community) but because it is inexorably developing into a global corporation. Community theatre, even in its most reactionary, nostalgic forms finds itself always in opposition to that development: in its most radical forms it must, however, also be able to make the connections to that wider context, even if it does so only to oppose it. Interculturalism is, then, both a pit-fall and a given for community theatre. To ignore its implications is to move towards the development of a siege culture.

In arguing as I have, I am well aware that I have made a sideways slip, from considering interculturalism in terms of cultural models (and specifically, in this context, of models of performance) to discussing it in larger social, political and economic constructs. In practice, it is hard not to do so, since concerns about interculturalism are never simply about protecting the purity of the form: the very existence and development of the performative model is a product of, and affected by, these larger constructs. In one sense, then, interculturalism can be seen less as a problem facing community theatre than as its most central subject matter: it cannot be ignored, it must be faced and it must, ultimately, be made use of.

Indeed, Bharucha himself does not write trying somehow to turn the clock back, acknowledging that in the modern, and even more in the postmodern world, interculturalism is as unstoppable as the tide, as demonstrated by King Canute to his courtiers. The second half of his book is given over to describing and analysing his and Manuel Lutgenhorst's experiment with situating the same one-woman, wordless play, *Request Concert* (Franz Xaver Kroetz) 'within the cultural contexts and actual living conditions to be found in different parts of Asia' (Bharucha, 1993, p.5). Interventionist community theatre, in particular, lives continually with these problems. Harris invokes, as had Kershaw before her, Eugenio Barba's formulation of 'barter', in which the source and the target communities (to continue with Harris's terminology, with an awareness of its inappropriateness in a less T.I.E. context) give something to each other. In extending this notion of barter to community theatre, acknowledgement must be made of the extent to which both Bharucha and Barba are, more or less explicitly, invoking a model of 'community' as the base from which barter may or may not take place; but in talking quite firmly about interventionist community theatre practice, it is clear that the process of bartering is not simply either a peripheral or a major source of worry - it is the very point of the exercise.

In community theatre practice, there is always the possibility of the 'target' audience becoming literally that, simply a sitting duck to be proselytised at. In good community theatre - and all the essays in this excellent collection articulate, in their very different ways, good practice - inter-action and mutual learning are essential. For the relationship between the community project and the community audience to have any real point, it must be a dialectical one, in which the situation as it is and the situation as it might be, the 'source' and the 'target', can arrive at some kind of synthesis. To achieve this *is* a form of bartering, for to effect change to some degree or other, at a personal or more general level, is always the aim of interventionist community theatre, which is at its most effective when barriers are being questioned and assumptions re-examined.

John Bull

## References

Ayckbourn, Alan (1982), *Ten Times Table*, in *Joking Apart and Other Plays*, Harmondsworth: Penguin.

Bharucha, Rustom (1993), *Theatre and the World: Performance and the Politics of Culture,* London: Routledge.

Hoggart, Richard (1992), 'Foreword', in Pamela Dellar (ed.), *People Make Plays: Aspects of Community Theatre in Hull Since 1955,* Beverly: Highgate.

Jellicoe, Ann (1987), *Community Plays: How to Put them On,* London: Methuen.

Kershaw, Baz (1992), *The Politics of Performance: Radical Theatre as Cultural Intervention,* London: Routledge.

McGrath, John (1981), *A Good Night Out: Popular Theatre: Audience, Class and Form,* London: Eyre Methuen.

Williams, Raymond (1976), *Keywords,* London: Fontana.

# The Contributors

**Peter Billingham** is Principal Lecturer and Subject Leader for Drama Studies at Bath Spa University College. He is also a dramatist with a growing reputation, making his full London debut with *Perfection* directed by Nadine Hanwell in 2003. One of his two most recent plays, *Blighty an anti-parable* (2004) has been invited into dramaturgical development by Talawa, the British Black and Asian theatre company. Peter Billingham's teaching and research specialist areas are the plays of Edward Bond, touring British community theatre 1939-53 and contemporary British and American television drama. His two most recent publications were *Sensing the City through Television* (Intellect 2000) and *Theatres of Conscience* (Routledge Harwood 2002). He has also been invited to write an essay on issues surrounding the ideological representations of gay sexuality in *Queer as Folk* (Channel 4/Red Productions) for a collection of essays on contemporary television drama to be published by Manchester University Press in 2005.

**John Bull** is Professor of Film and Drama at the University of Reading. He has published widely, mostly in the field of modern and contemporary theatre and drama (including *New British Political Dramatists* and *Stage Right: Crisis and Recovery in Contemporary British Mainstream Theatre*), and post-Restoration Theatre (including *Vanbrugh and Farquhar*). He has edited a volume of Howard Brenton's early plays, and is working on a six volume project, *British and Irish Dramatists Since World War II*, the third volume of which has just been published. The author of three produced plays, one a musical adaptation of Alfred Jarry's *Ubu* plays, he has also directed many contemporary and classic plays. In Easter 2004, he organised a highly successful international conference at the University of Reading, *Political Futures: Alternative Theatre in Britain Today*, some of the proceedings of which will be incorporated into a forthcoming volume of essays. He is a past chair of the Standing Conference of University Drama Departments, and is currently working on a book on politics and theatre in post-war Britain.

**Bill McDonnell** is currently Director of Drama in the Department of English Literature at the University of Sheffield. In 1980, following five years coordinating community theatre programmes at Chesterfield College of Art, he joined Roland Muldoon's CAST theatre company as an actor and writer. In 1983 he left CAST, and co-founded Sheffield Popular Theatre (1983-1992). He went on in 1984 to set up Theatreworks with John Goodchild. Between 1984 and 2000 they worked to develop forms of community based activist theatre in the inner city estates of Sheffield. These theatres belonged to a developing left theatre movement that was defined by an emphasis on positioning, on a 'politics of process', and on the interplay between theatre and activism, acting and action. Performers were drawn from working class communities who were resisting the Thatcher administrations, and theatre became a form of cultural activism. One of their most important relationships was with groups such as Belfast Community Theatre, the subject of his contribution. In 1996 he began a doctorate at Sheffield University based on this work. Since 2002 he has been a full time lecturer, responsible for a range of practice led modules, and is director of Acting Together, the university's Theatre in Education group. Bill McDonnell is currently working with Dominic Shellard on a report on the social impact of theatre for the Independent Theatre Council, and writing a book on the history of left wing theatres since 1979.

**Carole Christensen** is a British born drama teacher based in Copenhagen, Denmark. She has worked with educational drama and amateur theatre in both Sweden and Denmark with people of all ages. Since 1992 her work has been mainly in cross-cultural groups, where she has used and developed drama activities to facilitate language learning and integration. She strongly believes in drama's interactive potential for enabling immigrants and refugees to adjust living to a new culture, and has published several articles about her work including 'Adaptation through theatre: exploring multi-culturalism with immigrants' in the book *Drama for Life: Stories of Adult Learning and Empowerment*.

**Gunduz Kalic** is Senior Lecturer and Course Director of Performing Arts at Bath Spa University College. Formerly, he was Artistic and Executive Director of Taking Liberties Theatre Company of Brisbane, Australia, which specialised in producing political theatre and theatre for non theatre-going audiences. This work included both extensive outback travel and some exploration of 'theatre on television' in conjunction with ABC-TV and Channel 9 Television. Previously, Kalic had been Co-Director of East 15 Acting School and Artistic Director of the Corbett Theatre, London; Senior Lecturer in and Course Coordinator of Theatre Arts at Northern Territory University (and Artistic Director of Territory North Theatre) in Darwin; Senior Visiting Instructor at the Toneel Academie in the Netherlands; Assistant Professor of Theatre at Simon Fraser University in Canada and Artistic Director and lead actor of several Turkish repertory theatre companies as well as several Turkish films. Kalic has trained a number of stars and numerous journeymen and women of the UK, Dutch and Australian stage and screen. He has directed nearly two hundred plays, devising and/or co-writing a number of these. Also, he has written many articles on arts policy and on the role of 'illusion-making' in politics and elsewhere for Australian newspapers. In his early (pre East 15) career Kalic served lengthy apprenticeships with both illiterate Anatolian itinerant wandering players and with Karolous Koun in Athens. Somewhat later, in the early stages of a long exile from Turkey after a piece of political theatre directed by him was closed down by the police, Kalic wandered Italy and France, spending considerable time with and sometimes working in the companies of Jean Louis Barrault, Roger Planchon, Eduardo de Fillipo and Ca Foscari. He regards the French neo-Brechtian approach as a particular formative influence upon him. Strongly interested in the relationships between performance and both public and everyday life, acting practice and stand-up comedy and media and theatre, Kalic has sought, above all perhaps, through extensive practice-as-research to explore the roots of theatre in 'playing'.

**Velda Harris** has lectured in HE since the early 1970s. She has contributed to BA, MA and PGCE courses in Drama, English and Drama Education. She has a passionate interest in theatre, and during an extended period at Sheffield Hallam University, worked in collaboration with professional theatre practitioners from the Crucible Theatre on degree courses which included elements of community theatre; and directed annual productions for students and the general public, several of which were performed at the Crucible Studio. After three years in Hong Kong, during which she worked in a Vietnamese Refugee Camp, wrote and performed plays based on Amnesty case histories, devised plays on local topics with children from Chinese Government schools, contributed to INSET courses and to courses run by the Curriculum Studies Department of HKU, she returned to UK to work, briefly at Bretton Hall, and then in the Education Department at the Central School of Speech and Drama. There she was able to develop her interest in community theatre by expanding a course unit in the BA Drama and Education to include placements, not only in British mainstream and special schools, but also in educational venues abroad. These projects included a regular commitment to performances and workshops in displaced people's camps in Azerbaijan, a drama in second language teaching project in a primary school in Sicily, and projects in an orphanage and primary school in Ghana. It is the first of these projects that inspired the chapter in this book. Velda is currently employed as a part-time tutor in the Education Studies department at Sheffield University.

**John Salway** is Joint Projects Manager for 'Sheffield Popular Arts',, a community performance company. He continues to work on a range of Sheffield-based community theatre and TIE ventures – most recently a project on sexual health involving forum theatre called 'The Morning After'. He is also writing for theatre, film and TV more widely as well as journalism and history. He was the winner in August 2004 of the Lambeth Archives' inaugural History Writing Competition with a monograph on the causes of the Brixton Riots 1981-5, which will be published in May 2005.

# A Good Night Out on the Falls Road: Liberation Theatre and the Nationalist Struggle in Belfast 1984-1990

Bill McDonnell

## Introduction

> The experience of theatre starts long before the curtain rises and the play begins. Our theatre exists in the world in which we live, and our theatre experience, shaped by that world, rises from it and returns to it. The world of theatre is not sufficient unto itself. (Himani Bannerji)

Two continuities have defined the historical relationship between Britain and Ireland. The first is that of coloniser and colonised, a relationship underpinned by a deep and reflexive racism. The second has been the centrality of terror as a linchpin of the state's response to nationalist irredentism. The Earl of Pembroke, who landed at Bannow Bay near Waterford in 1167, set the precedent. Finding that the Irish were, understandably, less than willing to cede their land, he ordered the arrest of local leaders. Their arms and legs were systematically broken, and they were flung into the sea. As the historian Simon Schama notes dryly, 'The terror worked.' (Schama, 2000, p. 148) Eight hundred years later Britain has had more judgements bought against it for torture and breach of human rights than any other western nation. All have centred on its occupation of the north of Ireland.[1] Irish culture has mediated these continuities of oppression. During the 'Troubles', that strangely anodyne term for the latest period of republican insurgency, 1969-1997, culture was again foregrounded as a site of resistance and liberation.[2] Theatre was part of this resistance, and my essay deals with the work of two groups, Belfast Community Theatre and the Belfast People's Theatre. Both were based in the nationalist Ballymurphy estate in West Belfast. My knowledge of their work is based upon a relationship that was first and foremost a practical and political relationship, mediated through theatre exchanges, workshops, letters and interviews. During the period, I worked in the inner city estates of Sheffield with John Goodchild. This work, based on Freirean principles, and committed to the generation of 'amateur' theatres within popular campaigns and movements, was the basis of our dialogue with the Belfast groups.

Any study of cultural activism in the north of Ireland must necessarily conjure with the narrative of Republicanism within British political discourse. The attacks committed by the IRA on the British mainland have shaped popular perceptions of the nationalist struggle.[3] A highly effective partnership between state and mass media in the period 1969-1997 prevented the British public from accessing even the most notionally objective assessment of the British army's prosecution of its role.(Curtis, 1984) The result has been that the legitimate grievances of the nationalist people as a whole have been overlooked. The concern of this study is with the experiences of those people. That is to say, with those who did not bear arms, but who lived in an apartheid statelet, and whose communities became a violent laboratory for British counter insurgency methods. These theatres were a response to this history, and so I have fore grounded this history and the voices of those who endured it and sought to transform it. Critical writing is always a social and dependant act. The understandings that these experiences may bring do not belong to me, but to a collective and courageous enterprise.

## The Political Context

If Belfast Republicanism has an epicentre, then it is the Ballymurphy estate in West Belfast. Bounded by the Whiterock Road on one side, and by the Loyalist Spring Martin estate on two more, and protected at its base by the Falls Road, the area produced and lost more IRA volunteers than any other district in the north. It was the birthplace of Gerry Adams, future President of Sinn Fein; but also of Andy Tyrie, who was to become one of Loyalism's most feared killers. It was an estate that, long before the 'Troubles', had a reputation for social disorder and entrenched poverty. In his autobiography, Gerry Adams remembers the 'Murph' as being 'badly built, badly planned, and lacking in facilities.' (Adams, 1996, p. 5) Although Ballymurphy was a mixed community in the 1950s, by 1969 most Protestant families had moved to the nearby Springvale estate. Springfield Road, which separates the two estates, would become one of the most violent and notorious flash points of the 'Peace Line'.

The conflict in the north of Ireland was successfully naturalised by the British state as a sectarian struggle, with the British government as the neutral peace broker caught between tribal factions. For republicans and the British left, however, it was a neo-colonial conflict, whose religious and cultural dimensions (powerful and real), masked more fundamental contentions about the nature of Irish statehood, and the political identity of its people. Billy Mitchell of the Ulster Volunteer Force (U.V.F.) famously remarked that 'no one's getting shot over transubstantiation or Mary worship.' (Stevenson, 1996, p. 24)

It was a conflict rooted in the conjunction of three complex historical processes: (1) the eight hundred year old colonial relationship between Britain and Ireland, with its dominant themes of terror and the suppression of Irish nationalism; (2) the establishment of the apartheid Orange statelet and its institutional oppression of the catholic population from 1921; and (3) the industrial development of Belfast, with its concomitant exploitation of both the Protestant and Catholic working class. The Union was a capitalist and imperial construct, which maintained its power and interests through the agency of sectarianism, creating communal tensions that came to disguise deeper issues around class and nationhood. Mitchell again:

> The business people were mostly unionist...if you were a Catholic, you were being punished for your disloyalty, and we Protestants were being exploited for our loyalty...once you started to complain about your wages and your working conditions, you were promptly told, if you don't like it there's a hundred Catholics out in the street that will take your job tomorrow. (Stevenson, 1996, p. 76)

These experiences produced powerful and defensive communal relationships and belief systems. The image of fanatical neo-Marxist ideologues wielding Kalshnikovs in the cause of Connolly and Irish Freedom that came to characterise the IRA, was a myth.

For the most part the paramilitaries on both sides were motivated by more down to earth, immediate and communal necessities. Brendan Hughes, who was to have the role of supervising the second Hunger Strike of 1981, reflects this powerfully:

> I was a Catholic, and I seen the Catholic community under attack. My whole reason for joining the Provisionals at that time was not to bring about a thirty-two county democratic socialist republic, and *I had no ideology at that time*. We were a reactive force. (Stevenson, 1996, p. 36: my italics)

This response was echoed within Protestant communities. Ron McMurray of the U.V.F. notes that:

> one of the main motives for a lot of people was that you doing something for your community, in that we perceived an attack on our community, or on our identity. (Stevenson, 1996,p. 22)

This stress on the lack of ideological and political coherence in the early phase has been well documented. (Toolis, 1995; Kelley, 1982) Indeed, Gerry Adams has argued that the civil rights movement of 1968-69 had no agenda beyond the ending of discrimination in employment, and the securing of universal suffrage in local elections. (Adams, pp. 93-94) In that sense the movement was, argues Adams, part of an international moment, which linked Belfast and Derry to Prague and Paris, and to Saigon and Berkeley. It was the violence of the sectarian state's response, and which included shootings and the wholesale burning out of Catholic families on the Lower Falls, which ignited latent republican aspirations, and brought the fact of partition into sharp focus. The ensuing war drew upon, and deepened, the ideological, religious and cultural continuities that defined the two communities. This is not to evade the ideological tensions that marked debate within either republicanism or loyalism, but to underline the dominant reality of a grass roots solidarity that was deep, potent and historically durable.[4] This reflexive solidarity was the key to the IRA's ability to engage the British army for some 30 years. It saw itself as a community army, 'a people's army', which was resurrected in 1970 as a defence force against loyalist and state sponsored attacks on the catholic community. (Adams, 1986, pp. 63-69) The consequence of the IRA's activity was that the nationalist community became universally suspect. The goal of British counter-insurgency was the isolation of this army 'physically and psychologically from its civilian support.' (Pilkington, 1994, p. 35) To achieve this objective it utilised a range of repressive measures, including harassment, mass internment, beatings, legalised assassination, intimidation, torture, the wrecking of homes, and the separation of families. Ballymurphy was, until 1994, a war zone.

## A Popular Culture for a Popular Struggle

Obliged to sustain themselves as the political price for their perceived (and unacceptable) communal loyalties (to the IRA), the nationalist peoples constructed a de facto alternative state. This state within a state had its own army, police force, and cultural and educational networks. The theatre derived from this political and cultural infrastructure. For Joe Reid, community activist and founder member of Belfast Community Theatre, the relationship was absolute:

> Within the struggle for socialism, the arts, and theatre in particular are usually relegated to some sort of aesthetic void, removed from the mainstream of political activity. I believe this to be a fundamental mistake. Theatre, like all the arts, must be part of the overall political consciousness building which has to develop side by side with the political struggle.[5]

At the hub of the educational and cultural work was Springhill Community House in Ballymurphy, and Conway Mill on the Falls Road. Surrounded when I first went there in 1986 by boarded-up buildings, and approached across debris of concrete and glass, Springhill House was the home of Father Des Wilson and Sister Noelle Ryan. This remarkable three storey council house was a centre of education and healing for the war torn community.[6] In the small living areas of the house, some 300 adults and children a week came to attend education classes, formal and informal. The front room where visitors slept was also a classroom, church, and theatre. Goodchild and I performed there, between couch and fireplace. At Conway Mill, the network had access to more classrooms, a small theatre, a canteen and meeting spaces.

While the educational work was based on the liberation pedagogy of Paulo Freire, the spiritual dimension of the struggle was nourished by liberation theology.[7] The Catholic Church's support for the status quo, its use of the pulpit to attack nationalists while remaining largely uncritical of the military's actions, was a deep wound within the community. The struggle, then, was conceived as a dual one, embracing church and state. Liberation theology was inseparable from the nationalist project. The iconography of the republican movement reflected this intersection of armed struggle and radical theology. Bobby Sands, the Hunger Striker, depicted on murals with his unkempt beard and long hair, wrapped in a stained blanket and surrounded by brutal guards, was readily taken for the suffering Christ of Hope.

## Belfast Community Theatre

Drawn from the Ballymurphy, Twinbrook and Andersontown estates of West

Belfast, Belfast Community Theatre attracted individuals for whom the theatre served a range of needs. There were those who, like Reid, saw it as a political vehicle, a means of conscientization and mobilisation, for others it offered the simple opportunity to act, for others still it was a refuge, a source of comradeship, care and support. These were ordinary people in an extraordinary situation. They would insist on the concomitant ordinariness of theatre.[8] In the period the group was developing, Reid had started a three-year BA in English and Drama at Jordanstown University. It was there that he met lecturer Michael Klein. A New Yorker, Klein brought to his teaching a history of antiracist action and activism in the anti Vietnam and Black Rights' campaigns. He had worked for Luther King's organisation. Klein introduced Reid to the work of Piscator and Brecht, and to European and American underground films and writings. What Reid found in Klein was an empathy with the working class community that was absent from the rest of the academy. Klein encouraged Reid to write, and become involved in the theatre process as it evolved up to 1987. The result was a rich mix, which brought to bear on a politicised working-class theatre the influence of a cosmopolitan radicalism.

The initial group of Joe Reid, Marie McKnight and Jim and Pat McGlade came from the Springhill network. Jim McGlade was a playwright who would write material for the group and act when necessary. Indeed, the first play the group performed was not directly about the nationalist experience. *Oh Gilbert!*, written by Jim McGlade, explored attitudes towards people with learning difficulties. The production was successful and brought in Tony Flynn and Gerard McLaughlin to form a core of six performer/writers. Other activists would join for specific projects. McKnight:

> People come into the theatre through working together in other community groups. It's very much a community-based group that tries to deal with the issues. Each recognised a need within their communities for things to be said on social issues, on community issues. (Belfast Community Theatre, 1986)

This organic relationship produced a critical dialogue between community and theatre which was central to its value, as Reid notes:

> Theatre must stand at the heart of struggle, and the tensions performed on the stage cannot be allowed to be abstracted from the reality of the audience's experience. Our community is our stage...Theatre is not about abstract issues or arguments about this or that theory; theatre in this context is about life and death. (Belfast Community Theatre, 1986)

Reid's comments are not melodramatic but precise. If Thatcherism had brought social conflict to Britain, it had intensified the existing crisis in the north of Ireland. The death of ten republican volunteers in hunger strikes between April and October 1981, brought her especial opprobrium, reflected in the IRA's assassination attempt at the 1984 Tory party conference.[9] The Hunger Strike had two effects. In the longer term, Sands' election to the British parliament would mark the beginning of republicanism's dual political and military strategy.[10] In the short term, it led to an intensification of violence on the streets. In 1981 alone 29,601 plastic bullets were fired by crown forces on the streets of the north: more than in the previous eight years taken together. (Ashley, 1985, p. 173) Sinn Fein's new political strategy led to a growth in community-based politics and cultural activism. Belfast Community Theatre was, says Reid, an example of this.

At the core stood people who were very, very committed and politically motivated, and who had, if you like, a particular vision of people's entitlement, people's rights. And although in the scheme of things people may argue the right to write a play is not a big right, to us it was a fundamental right because it stood at the very core of the struggle that was going on in this country.[11]

One of Belfast Community Theatre's responses was what they would term 'Mixed Bags'. These were cultural events, sometimes spanning whole days, and staged at the theatre in Conway Mill. Marie McKnight offered some sense of the range and richness of the work:

> Lady Gregory's plays had been written in the 1920s. We adapted them and changed the language a bit, to make them a bit more modern. But they were as relevant today as they were in the 20s. And they actually dealt with the supergrass issue, which is by no means a new thing, you know. We did a Brecht *On Education*, a piece on George Jackson, Thomas Jefferson, James Connolly, Willie Mandela. (Belfast Community Theatre, 1986)

These latter were called *The Oxygen Plays*, and were meant, says McKnight, to 'bring the air of truth, of understanding to the community.' (Belfast Community Theatre, 1986) The 'Brecht' she mentions was a reworking of the plot of *The Mother*.

In Belfast Community Theatre's version, the focus is upon Maeve, a cleaner, whose brother has been arrested by the British army. Driven from her flat by the Unionist Housing Executive, she is taken to the house of the local teacher, Peter. While Peter disapproves of the nationalist struggle, he does need a housekeeper, and he agrees to employ Maeve. In the second scene, several neighbours arrive at the house while Peter is at work. On a blackboard they begin to write single words: democracy; socialism; Ireland, and at this point, Peter returns. He is angered to find a political meeting taking place in his kitchen, but is persuaded by Maeve to teach them. Arguing that education would be wasted, given their social position, he nonetheless begins to write the word 'buy' on the board. They protest and ask for the spelling for 'worker'. He refuses, telling them that they are going too fast, and that 'buy' is a simple word and, in this society, a more useful one. To this, one retorts, 'Class struggle is simpler.' When Peter tells them that reading and class struggle are separate things altogether, they take over the teaching themselves. Crowded around the blackboard, the neighbours work to construct the spellings they need: words that correspond to their daily experiences. What we have within this scenario is a theatrical restating of Freire's concept of literacy as:

> an event calling forth the critical reflection of both the learners and educators: the literacy process must relate *speaking the word* to *transforming reality* and to man's [sic] role in this transformation. (Freire, p. 31)

This dramatic image of the displacement of the teacher by the student, of authority by popular control, of statist ideology by a socialist worldview, mirrored developments within the community. *On Education* both celebrated and reinforced the grass roots education system being developed through Springhill. In addition, it carried an emphasis on class as the ground of identity, and of class struggle as the fulcrum of change. This stress on class politics would be the most important theoretical and ideological contribution Belfast Community Theatre made to nationalist discourse.

The group also acted as a 'Living Newspaper'. Experiences in the north would be contextualised in montages drawing on struggles in South Africa, Chile, Nicaragua, India, and Britain. Ghettoised by the war, confined by military occupation, the plays emphasised the universal nature of these *structures of experience*.[12] The theatre placed the immediate experiences of their community in the context of a global movement for civil rights and self-determination. Again, it is of little moment here whether we agree that this was a liberation struggle; it was how the group perceived their work:

> the idea was there that this was a part of a national liberation statement, if you want, that echoed across the world. It was not something that belonged solely to Ireland. It wasn't Irish. This was a human experience that happened to be happening in Ireland. And so the link was made. (Reid, 1998)

Following the success of these plays, and with a desire to broaden both the scope and context for their work, the group decided to use theatre as a means to carry their people's experiences onto the stages of the mainstream.

## Radical Theatre as Cultural Trojan Horse

If the early eighties represented a seismic moment in the history of the republican movement and the beginning of its slow, historic shift towards constitutional politics, it also marked the advent of a new tactic in the state's war against insurgency - the Supergrass. The IRA and the loyalist paramilitaries had always been vulnerable to informers. However, the period after 1981 was to see, in the words of one of the more famous of them, Sean O'Callaghan, informing turned into a 'full blown system, and one of the main weapons in the state's armoury against the terrorist organisations.' (O'Callaghan, 1999, p. 177) It was this issue, and the terrible impact informing had on community cohesion, that led Belfast Community Theatre to take it as the theme for an intervention into the prestigious official Belfast Festival fringe programme for 1985. This annual event was offered to the world as proof that, despite a neo-colonial war in which significant proportions of the city's (working class) population had been killed, mutilated, traumatised or imprisoned, decency and all the other 'universal' values inhering in 'culture' survived.

Culture was a vital element of the apparatus of Ulsterisation instigated in 1976. Ulsterisation was a significant decision taken by the state to turn the war with the IRA from a neo-colonial conflict into an issue of internal law enforcement. IRA volunteers were no longer to be seen as soldiers but gangsters; their motives no longer political but pecuniary and anarchic. Against this violent and causeless anarchy (understood, with drunkenness and stupidity, as an issue of racial disposition) would be projected a constructed normality, which included the arts.

Within republican circles, then, there was a perception that culture had to become a more deliberate site of resistance. Writer and H block prisoner Eoghan MacCormaic had called for a policy of using literature as a means of 'corrupting the enemy's language, not just English, but the terminology and the built in assumptions on racism, sexism or class superiority.' (Pilkington, p. 136) This neo-Gramscian analysis was reflected in Belfast Community Theatre's next intervention. For the group set out in 1985 to expose the mainstream theatre's collusion in the state's suppression of representations of nationalist experience. The vehicle chosen for this act of cultural 'entrism' was Samuel Beckett's *Eh Joe*. Reid:

> *Eh Joe* was a play about betrayal. We were in the supergrass period. There was a lot of betrayal. I use that in very guarded terms. But it was an issue. And I thought that the echoes in *Eh Joe*, the language in *Eh Joe*, we could tinker a bit with that. (Reid, 1998)

It is easy to see how the play resonated with the group and the community. It was a community surrounded by forts and 'listening posts'. Helicopters hovered over it twenty-four hours a day, taking photographs and recording conversations. M15 and M16 and Special Branch agents had infiltrated its organisations. It was riddled with *agent provocateurs* and informers. In such a climate Beckett's intensely private, internal hell of betrayal became for Belfast Community Theatre a possible metaphor for a generalised condition: that of the community as undifferentiated suspect. The insistent accusation of the voice in general is sharpened by the specific image:

> You're all right now, eh? ...No one can see you now...Why don't you put out that light? Say it now, Joe, no one' ll hear you...come on Joe, no one can say it like you...Look up, Joe, look up, we're watching you...And it's the worst...Isn't that what you said? ...The whisper...The odd word...Straining to hear...Brain tired squeezing... (From *Eh, Joe!*, an adaptation by Belfast Community Theatre of the original play by Samuel Beckett)

Confident that the community would feel these resonances, Belfast Community Theatre decided to go a step further, or rather two steps, the one formal, the other related to content. For the problem they faced was that Beckett's is a supremely aural aesthetic, which works on the ear not the eye. His characters' conflicts are also in the past. How were they to yank this aural drama of memory into the present? Within the innocent phrase 'played about with it', then, is caught what amounted to a total redefinition of the piece for the stage. Instead of Beckett's disembodied face (Joe) and voice (The Woman), the group placed the protagonist in a room around which he could move. He had a pallet in a corner, torn sheets to cover his head, and a table under which he could hide. Instead of the strictly set motions of the camera in the original, a spotlight marked the interstices in the text. This absolute rupture of the play's structure was extended to the text. In section 6, Beckett's words are excised, and in their place Belfast Community Theatre inserted the following:

> One phone call...that's all it took. Two meetings. Simple arrangements. What is her name, Joe? ...Where does her brother live? Tell us, Joe...A story about a bomb...Some rifles...The details don't matter...We'll fill them in...Information please...We'll fix you up with a new identity...Supply you with heroin...We'll take care of you...Across the water...University...Money...Nobody will know...One phone call...That's all it took, Joe...But what about me? What about our people, Joe?

Beckett's character is now a supergrass, his torment and language appropriated by the group. Talking of the changes they made, Reid explains the rationale for the work:

> The female character in it was calling Joe to account. That was what we were trying to say to people. You are responsible for your actions. You cannot Pontius Pilate yourself, and you may escape, but your escape is always going to be one of exile. If not physical exile, it's certainly going to be emotional exile because you've put a gap between you and your community which will never heal. And in the darkness of the night you hear 'Eh, Joe!' You hear the accusing voice. (Reid, 1998)

However, the reaction of the Festival audiences to *Eh Joe* was not one of horror at the violation of a community in a war zone only one mile away, but outrage at the violation of one of Ireland's canonical texts.

*Eh Joe* was an interesting act of cultural subversion. It neatly unpicked the 'apparatus's collusion, and its reflexive censorship of the minority voice. Nonetheless, it also marked the end of Belfast Community Theatre's experiments with existing texts, and with cultural *entrism*. For the next three years they would concentrate on new plays based on the nationalist experience. Important material for this work was to come from the prisons.

## The Prisons and the Community

At core of the Republican struggle were the prisoners. No important strategic or political action was ever taken without their assent. Within the H Blocks in this period there were two forms of theatrical activity.[13] The first was the writing and smuggling out of plays by inmates, and the second was the development of Forum-style dramas within the blocks. Pilkington offers a rare account of the role of the latter, whereby the rotation of prisoners as part of the 'red book' security process became the means by which sketches on republican events and issues were also 'rotated'. (Pilkington, p. 136) As the plays were passed around from wing to wing, they were, in the spirit, if not the methodology, of Boal's Forum Theatre, amended and developed in response to their audience's view of the issues. The plays were seen both as a means to mediate internal debate, and as a useful recruitment strategy for the IRA's analysis. Nearly a decade later, in 1994-95, theatre worker Tom Magill was to carry out similar experiments in the H blocks using Boal's Image Theatre techniques. (Magill, 1998, pp. 21-22)[14] However, it was the other area of prison theatre production, the writing of scripts, which was to offer material for the group. Written on toilet paper or cigarette papers, which were then smuggled out in cling film by mouth, scripts were carefully reconstituted outside, and offered to the group. To hold one of these scripts, a paper trail of minute and laboriously pencilled dialogue and stage directions, is to be brought once more against a politics of theatre that cannot be contained within, or evaluated against, existing analyses. One prison script, performed as part of a Mixed Bag at Conway Mill was *The Night Before Clontarf*. Written in 1984-5, it offers a fascinating example of how the prisoners' plays sought to intervene in the political processes outside.

## Night Before Clontarf

The play's actions are set in 1843, on the eve of a rally called by Daniel O'Connell's Repeal Association and the militant Young Irelanders. The success of O'Connell's campaign, framed in the Emancipation Act of 1829, had been bought at the cost of the disenfranchisement of the poorest Catholics, and the banning of his own association.[15] The Young Irelanders, the precursors of the IRA, were a response to this accommodation, arguing against O'Connell's pacifism, and urging armed struggle against the British.[16] Warned by the British authorities that the rally was deemed subversive and illegal, and would be crushed, O'Connell called it off. This 'caving in' to Westminster only served to sharpen the growing division in the movement between constitutional nationalism and physical force republicanism: a division which has remained to the present day the axis of the internal politics of Irish Nationalism. It was this division that the play took as its content. It is not so much a play as a series of dialogues. Five nationalists, who are on their way to Clontarf, meet at a tavern. Two are from O'Connell's movement, three are from the Young Irelanders. Over drinks, the five contest the legitimacy of their opposed positions. While the republican voice in the play, Cahir, is prepared to concede the commitment of the reformists, he counsels against taking small concessions for victories:

> CAHIR: I cannot agree that the disappointments come from military defeats. There is always some comfort in the knowledge that at least you tried. The real disappointment comes when you think you have won, and then suddenly discover that you have won nothing more than a moral victory. That is the danger of relying too much on moral force. Sometimes it takes real force to win real victories. (*Night Before Clontarf*: 1.i.)

The fear expressed here, of the absorption of revolutionary energies by constitutional processes, was real enough for hard liners within the IRA They could point to the ceasefire of 1975 as a moment where accommodation had almost led to the destruction of the movement. It also spoke to the heart of the debate taking place in 1986 within the Republican movement. For it was at their 1986 Ard Fheiseanna (annual conference) that Sinn Fein voted to end 70 years of abstentionism from the Republic's parliament, the Dail Eireann. It was a decision that signalled the beginning of the political shift within the movement towards the Adams/McGuinness axis. The Good Friday Agreement of 10 April 1998 was the outcome of their slow struggle to convince the movement that Irish unity could now be achieved through demography, and the increasingly explicit indication of the British state's desire to disengage.[17] *The Night Before Clontarf* was therefore deeply relevant. However, it was not *Clontarf*, but a script fragment dealing with interrogation and strip-searching which was to have the greatest creative impact. From this fragment, smuggled out in cling film, was to come their best-known and most powerful play, *Sign on the Dotted Line.*

In the post Hunger Strike period the nationalist community was, in Reid's words, going through a 'tremendous cultural and community trauma'. (Reid, 1998) In Maghaberry Women's jail, strip-searching, an examination of mouth, vagina and anus, had been introduced for all prisoners whenever they moved anywhere within or without the prison. Nationalist lawyers petitioned the European Court of Human rights over the issue and the Anti Strip Searching campaign was founded, based on an alliance between the H Block Committees, Sinn Fein and the Women's Centres. *Sign on the Dotted Line* was Belfast Community Theatre's contribution to the campaign. A performance of the play at Conway Mill on 18 March 1987 was my and Goodchild's practical introduction to the group's work. In the account that follows, I have drawn on both the unpublished text and on memory for the images made an intense impression. All quotations are from the unpublished script. By writing in the present tense I hope to approximate the immediacy that defines all performance.

## A Good Night Out on the Falls Road

Father Wilson drives us from Springhill House down to the Falls Road. On the way we encounter two army roadblocks. Security at the gates of the Mill complex is tight, and cameras check us while we wait for Des Wilson to be recognised. In the foyer we are checked again. Once at the Education floor we buy a cup of tea at the bar, where our money is waved away. We make our way into the theatre. The room is long and narrow, with a roughly constructed stage at one end. I note the number of children in the audience.

## Sign on the Dotted Line in Performance

From hidden speakers, the mute bass of the Congolese *Missa Luba* rises and then dies away. A single spot stage left lights a solitary figure who is seated upon the floor. His legs are crossed, and he leans forward, one hand holding an ankle. The image is held as he begins to sing. The song is Behan's *The Auld Triangle*. His voice is beautiful, clear and youthful. From the rear of the hall another voice joins in, deeper, more powerful. The duet encloses us, as past and present meet: the continuity of struggle, and of art's response to it, is implicit. In the image of the confined prisoner, Ireland finds its most potent metaphor.

## Scene One

The lights dim and then rise, creating a corridor of half light along the front of the stage. At each corner, down-stage right and left, a figure crouches and further back is the Narrator. As the play progresses it becomes apparent that she is audience guide, players' friend, prompt, alter ego and spare performer. In a mixture of Boal's 'Joker' system and Brechtian aesthetic, she is ubiquitous, detached, and omnipresent, calling the play's stylistic shifts into existence. She watches as the two figures begin to whisper across the space dividing them. One is busy ruling lines onto a small piece of toilet roll.

> KEVIN: Hurry up. Be careful. Are you ready?
>
> DONAL: Just a minute

A guard shouts in from stage left: 'Be quiet in there!' The two prisoners now whisper in Gaelic. Again the voice calls:

> VOICE: You pair shut up, or I'll have you both on report. And give up talking in that foreign babble.

This is enough to tell us that they are Republicans, and we experience the incongruity of the Irish language being referred to as 'foreign', and note the pejorative term 'babble'. The word of colonialists for 'native' tongues, it carries undertones of the subhuman, of infantilism. Language and the land are indivisible: the one is called for through the other. Repressing the use of one is an attempt to suppress the struggle for the other.

Why, Kevin now asks, are two prisoners accused of insurrection writing a play on toilet paper? What is the meaning of that response? And why do this under such difficult condition, risking beatings and solitary confinement? In order that our struggle is never forgotten, answers Donal. The two turn again to setting down the script painstakingly on the tiny piece of paper. The lights blackout.

## Scene Two

As the lights rise, the Narrator comes forward. The tone now is urgent and business like:

> NARRATOR: The scene is Ballymurphy. The time is the present. Tony Murphy's house was raided on a cold, damp morning at 5 a.m. under the infamous section 11

of the Emergency Provisions Act. He was then placed in a Landrover and taken to Castlereagh interrogation centre. Once in Castlereagh he was handed over to the Special Branch for interrogation. The Special Branch file on Tony Murphy included reports about him mixing with 'subversive types', including well known Ballymurphy Republicans Patsy Mulligan and Toni Tinnsley. This is Murphy's first time in Castlereagh. But there have been others there before him.

The lights change to a single spot. The Narrator moves into it. A tin whistle is heard. She begins to read a Bobby Sands' poem. Once again republican history reaches out and claims all individual experiences for its own.

NARRATOR:

I scratched my name but not for fame, upon the whitened wall,

Bobby Sands was here I wrote with fear, in awful shaky scrawl,

I wrote it low where eyes don't go, it was just to testify

That I am sane and not to blame should I come here to die.

The poem, simple and halting, is crucial to the unfolding of the drama - not only in its evocation of the Hunger Strike, but through the values it presents. The republican hero is revealed as vulnerable, fearful, and modest, yet he starved himself to death, privileging Irish freedom before his own life. As the last lines are spoken, a guard brings in Tony Murphy.

## Scene Three

The zone lighting, which is central to the play's aesthetic, now plays upon the rostra. Behind Tony, there is blackness. He is restless, fearful, breathing heavily, and the light intensifies his isolation. We hear voices and two Special Branch officers enter. They ignore Tony and sit down. One of them, Haddock, places a file on the table. He studies it, looks at Tony, studies the file again. The question when it comes is chatty, like a bank manager checking your financial needs:

HADDOCK: OK, let's see...hmmm...hmm...right...when did you join the Provos?

TONY: I'm not in the Provos.

(Haddock slams down the file, turns to McMullan.)

HADDOCK: Talk to him!

They claim to have evidence that Tony has consorted with known IRA volunteers, naming some local people he has chatted to in a pub. Did he know they were in the Provos? No, he didn't. They probably aren't. They tell him that his house is being raided. His elderly mother is there. If he co-operates she can be told where he is. He again protests his innocence. Haddock leave to check on the progress of the house raid. The pressure is drip-drip, the accusations, the house raid, and his mother. Tony's powerlessness is absolute. Interrogation works because it goes to the heart of our value system. What matters to us? For Tony it is love for his mother. In the space between this love, and his fear of what might be done to her, the interrogators do their work. Haddock rushes back in: they have found bullets in Tony's house. Who put them there? If Tony didn't, it can only mean one thing, his mother did. He denies this; they pressure him. They bang the table, shout, plead, accuse. Tony's head jerks from one to the other, seeking an anchor in this bewildering farce. The scenario is almost banal, B-movie stuff. Haddock pretends to lose his temper. He walks behind Tony, grabs his hair and yanks his head sharply back. He raises his fist and Tony cries out. McMullan pretends to shield his eyes as if he can't bear to see violence. It's ham acting: the police revue sketch. They are acting a script. Tony, they intimate, is a bad actor. He knows enough of the plot, but he won't take his cue. They offer now to leave him to think things over - to 'get his act together'. As they go Haddock offers him the final twist in the narrative they are all creating together:

> HADDOCK: I'll tell you what, Sonny, we're going to go for a cup of tea now. You have a good think to yourself while we're away, all right? We'll continue this when we get back. Mind you, it was a pity that your mother took that wee turn when our boys were searching the house. They had to call for the doctor. I hope you start co-operating because I wouldn't like to be held responsible for the consequences of interrogating a sick old woman.

They go. Tony sits shaking. We hear snatches of the *Old Triangle*. In the interrogation cell you are never alone: history, and its myths, crowd in and names that have been scratched on walls call to you.

McMullan re-enters with a deal to offer Tony. They're prepared to forget his non-existent Provo activities if he'll play a part for them. So Tony can go free, and his mother will be left alone, if he will inform against his community.

The interrogators now close in, physically and metaphorically. They lay a piece of paper on the table:

> MCMULLAN: Well, Tony, Mr Haddock and I have already prepared a statement. All you have to do is sign on the dotted line.

There is a long pause. McMullan holds a pen out to Tony, who turns and looks at it. They freeze. The lights black out.

We do not know what Tony chose, any more than we can know what choice anyone makes in the terrible loneliness of the interrogation cell. The play does not condemn those who sign, nor does it fete those who do not. The theatre does not invite judgement, but a complex and historically aware solidarity.

## Scene Four

A single spot lights down stage left. A young girl walks into the light. The spot lights only her face, so that it looks as if it were suspended above the earth:

> GIRL: My name is Maria and I was fourteen the day they stopped me growing to be fifteen...They told my mummy and my daddy I had been throwing stones at them, that I was a threat to their armoured cars...I was only going to the shop...I can't forgive the papers or the men who came on TV and said how regrettable it was that I had to die, such a waste of life they said...but did I have to die? What harm could I have done to them?

So begins a monologue which stands as a memorial for the sixteen children aged under sixteen who have been killed by plastic bullets in the north of Ireland. Children like Carol Anne Kelly, aged twelve, shot on 12 May 1981, or Julie Livingstone, aged fourteen, whose face was removed by a plastic bullet on 22 May 1981. The monologue's combination of innocence and bewilderment, of forgiveness and childish musings is devastating. The light fades.

## Scene Five

The Narrator moves forward. We are about to witness the second interrogation, that of Patsy Mulligan. McMullan appears, dragging her by the arm. She resists and he is forced to push her into the centre chair. They reprise their mockery of human intercourse.

> MCMULLAN: Well Patricia, or is it Pat?
>
> *(She says nothing, staring straight ahead, impassive and mute.)*
>
> MCMULLAN: Well, I'm Detective Sergeant McMullan and this is Detective Constable Haddock.
>
> HADDOCK: Oh, Patsy and I go back a long way. Isn't that right, Pat?
>
> MCMULLAN: Well now, Patsy, what would you like us three to talk about?

Once more there is this grotesque inversion, as if Patsy had called them in for therapy. She says nothing, indeed, the motive power of this scene is her silence, her refusal to engage. She is being held for seven days under the P.T.A. It happens regularly. They get up, circle her, probing, stroking her hair, touching her breasts and thigh. She flinches, goes to push the hand away, but stops herself. She stares ahead. The innuendo is aggressive, sexual:

> HADDOCK: There'll be no fucking about with your Provo boyfriends this weekend. Mind you, from what we hear, you'll be missing it a hell of a lot more than they will.

They lean towards her. Black out.

## Scene Six

The lights rise down stage right. It is a street. Two women meet and exchange chit-chat. One mentions Patsy Mulligan - she has been lifted again. It becomes clear Patsy has been leading the campaign against strip-searching. She is a militant, and they admire her. Her struggle is theirs, it is symptomatic, historical, and the community owns it. It is also, and this is now becoming apparent, a struggle about the double oppression of women. The lights fade.

## Scene Seven

We are back in the interrogation room. Haddock jumps to his feet, screaming into Patsy's face, banging the table:

> HADDOCK: I'm biased? Sure, didn't Murphy tell us earlier that Tinsley and this bitch here were going out to shoot policemen. Yes, you! Answer me! I'm talking to you!

He pulls at her blouse, which rips. She grabs at it. McMullan moves across and pretends to restrain him. The double act is in full play now. We also note the reference to Tony Murphy. Did he sign? We do not know, and nor does Patsy. What we can see is the ripped blouse, the violent gestures, two men alone with one woman. Patsy stays immobile and silent. Haddock hits her, tears at her hair, screams abuse, and then storms out. The hatred is palpable. Silence. Patsy is still, McMullan stares at her and sits down. He feigns concern; one parent for another. What will happen to Patsy's little girl if she is jailed?

> MCMULLAN: What age would she be now? Two? Three? That's the age my own wee one is. You know she nearly screams the place down every time my wife leaves her; she can hardly go to the toilet without the child crying after her. For Christ's sake Patsy, wake up! If you're not worried about yourself, think of your child!

He gets up. Patsy hasn't moved. Her eyes stare ahead; her face is closed against him. He threatens her with Maghaberry. He sets out in detail the realties of strip-searching. She is silent. He goes. The Narrator steps forward now, acting as Patsy's alter ego. Now we hear her inner turmoil, her face contorts with the effort of repressing emotion: the danger of weakness in front of interrogators:

> ALTER EGO: Christ, I hate those bastards! Scum, who do they think I am? That I would sign other people into this hell-hole? ...God, what about wee Sinead...her granny'll be putting her to bed around now, and she'll probably forget to give her that old blue jumper...it's full of holes but she can't sleep without it. She's so shy. If they put her in one of those homes she'll be so distracted.

Patsy calls on the two forces which shape her life: Catholicism and Republicanism, God and a United Ireland, in whose name the present must surrender to the future. She is totally distraught. Haddock comes back in. He screams into her face. She is facing conspiracy to murder. Patsy is going to Maghaberry for life.

## Scene Eight

We hear the *Missa Luba* Sanctus. The stage is in total darkness, except for a low light on the Narrator. She is again Patsy's alter ego. A loud voice is heard:

> VOICE: Right, strip!
>
> ALTER EGO: Silent young woman
>
> Alone, so forlorn
>
> Awaits in subjection
>
> No clothes adorn
>
> VOICE: Come on, get them off! We haven't got all day you know!
>
> ALTER EGO: Maiden there standing
>
> No pity knows
>
> Waiting just waiting
>
> Her nakedness shows
>
> VOICE: Right, you bitch, let's have the sanitary towel!

So the scene unfolds, with this counterpoising of the simple haunting beauty of the poetry, and the banalities and cruelties of the voices. It is an evocation of ritual defilement which speaks of martyrdom and holy solitariness: Christ amongst his tormentors, Connolly strapped to his chair in the cold light of dawn, Sands defiant in his cell. There is raucous laughter and the light slowly fades.

## Scene Nine

After the noise and brutality of the interrogation and the still, painful dignity of the last scene, Patsy's entrance into Maghaberry is almost domestic in its ease and warmth. After the corruption of closeness and touch, it is also a celebration of love, of caring, of women in solidarity. Once again, there is the deliberate interplay of styles. The scene opens with three women sitting in a semicircle front stage centre, talking. Patsy enters but stands unnoticed. The women make room for her and ask solicitously about her experience. They allow her for the first time to acknowledge the horror of what she has been through. Patsy breaks down. They soothe her, but make clear the consequences of her choice. Strip-searching, humiliation, and abuse will be the condition of their lives together. The scene ends in affirmation:

> ROSA: You're all right now, love. You can trust us. We're all in the same boat. They may be able to frame us...to humiliate us...

PATSY: But by God, and by Christ, they will never, never break us!

The light focuses upon her, with her clenched fist raised in a salute to the audience. The lights cut out.

## Scene Ten

Darkness. The Kyrie from *Missa Luba* begins. Two lights illuminate Tony and Patsy. They begin a hymnal to the Irish struggle, locating the specific suffering in the universal fight against oppression. Voices from the audience join in:

VOICE: Let freedom ring from the mountains of Kerry to the hills of Antrim, from Soweto to Greenham Common!

PATSY: Irish men and Irish women, in the name of god and the dead generations...

TONY: We declare the right of the people of Ireland to the ownership of Ireland. We declare the right of the peoples of the world to live free from poverty, tyranny and fear...

PATSY: And freedom from imprisonment and degradation...

TONY: As Connolly...

PATSY: And Countess Markeiwicz were imprisoned before us.

VOICE: Our day will come!

ALL: Venceramos! Our day will come! Our day will come!

The music rises now to a crescendo as the Kyrie comes to its conclusion. The lights snap out. There is silence. As the applause rings out the group come forward to bow, and then melt into an audience from which they came, and to which they always return.

## The Making of Sign on the Dotted line

*Sign* was the product of a deeply political and communal reflex. To place this in a more concrete context, here is how Paula accounted for the play's genesis:

> The beginning of the play was written by two men in the H blocks of Long Kesh. It was smuggled out of the gaol on small cigarette papers and tissue papers, and it was passed onto the community theatre. We built our play around that. We felt that there were a lot of issues that needed to be raised, such as strip-searching, such as plastic bullets and so on. So four women members of the group got together for maybe a week in each other's houses. We sat around and we talked to women. We invited along ex-prisoners. Women who'd been through strip-searching, who'd been

through interrogation, who could relive, if you like, what they'd been through. Then we talked about what they'd said. We talked out a script into a tape recorder, and then picked out the best parts.

> That's how the whole second section dealing with Patsy was written. The women members of the group felt it was really important to bring out the strip-searching issue through women. The play grew around that. There was the section on plastic bullets written by Joe. The introduction and ending was written separately.
>
> (From an interview given by Belfast Community Theatre to the author, Sheffield, October 1987.)

The statement encapsulates the process. The theatre is created in a cell, a kitchen, a community space, a theatre and in one man's head. It arrives through the agency of cigarette papers smuggled in mouths from a prison, a tape recorder, paper and pen, debate and argument. It is begun by men, and taken forward with a deeper agenda by women. It is part reportage, part text, and part improvisation. A particular issue, interrogation, becomes a prism through which other experiences are refracted. However, while the script exists, and can be re-interpreted, what cannot be reproduced is this process, the collective 'method' by which the play came to be made. It was a method conjured out of the interaction of people with an unstable reality, and negotiated amid politically created limitations on access, resources, space and time. Belfast Community Theatre demonstrated a politics of improvisation that moves us beyond notions of devising, to embrace both the sequence of human activities that produced the script, and the means by which nationalists survived an unpredictable and hostile reality.

## 'Writing' the Script

At the beginning there was no 'plot'. It was through the practical testing out of script fragments and the counterpoising of images that the group arrived at a narrative structure. However, it was a consensus that was achieved through passionate and tense debate.

> That isn't to say that there aren't tensions. There are. There's a lot of disagreements. Because it's so important to us. We all feel very strongly about this. (Belfast Community Theatre, 1987)

The level of republican commitment in the group ranged from passive support to those who, like Paula and Maraid, were extremely active. It was these two women who provided the script with its visceral power and its stringent politics. A key advisor in making sure the play reflected the reality of interrogation and strip-searching was Maraid Farrell, later to be shot dead by members of the SAS in Gibraltar in 1988.[18]

Influenced by Brecht's theories, Reid and Klein insisted that each image or script offered by the group should be constructed into a scene or scenario that would be rehearsed as a stand-alone. 'If it worked on its own, it worked', Reid notes. Only when the different elements were in place did the issue of structure arise, of a way of cohering what Reid calls a 'stylistic mish-mash.' The Narrator, a figure who was conceived as an historical interlocutor, was the formal device that they used. Reid comments:

> We weren't concerned with 'form': what we were concerned with was getting the message across. What medium suited the message? (Reid, 1998)

The play was in itself a statement about this process, about the right to mobilise all forms or styles in service of the ideas and feelings being presented. As noted, some sections of the text arrived in developed form. The Plastic Bullet scene, which Reid wrote alone, was one example. Sections of the interrogation scene with Patsy were also well advanced before rehearsals. The rehearsal was a means to test and refine these. Direction was shared. Local people coming into the Mill for classes or a drink would be invited to watch rehearsals and to offer their responses. This continuous interplay between reception and production was a key aspect of the creative activity. It was a process of refinement using improvisation within very defined parameters.

While the group welcomed any consciousness raising achieved in people such as ourselves, their most intense focus was on breaking a barrier which existed *within* their own community, between those who had been through interrogation, and those who had not. For after the terrible isolation of the cells, many prisoners felt unable to convey - even to loved ones - what they had been through. Paula again:

> No one can ever understand what you personally go through. It's like a woman being raped. No one can understand what she really experienced. So a lot of people who have been though interrogation, who have been through strip-searching...even after the event is over...after they are out of prison...they still feel isolated.

The analogy with rape underlines the fact that *Sign on the Dotted Line* is also a play about patriarchy, and about the double oppression of women within the nationalist community. There is no doubt that the show helped open up a debate on these experiences, providing both therapeutic support for the women and supporting mobilisation against the practices it excoriated. As Brecht noted, 'true A effects are of a combative character': epic theatre was not supposed to stimulate theoretical discussions, but praxis. (Willett, 1986, p. 77) The play also had an important educational role for the young men and women who were entering the 'harassment zone' of age 16-35, and for whom such interrogations and choices would soon be a reality. Augusto Boal's categorisation of such theatre as monologic: of the audience *per se* as 'immobilised' by its passive relationship to the stage's action, would not be recognised by Belfast Community Theatre. For the group, as for Brecht, the audience in a situation of insurgency is a dynamic player, and is engaged by history before aesthetics make any claim. Uptal Dutt, the charismatic impresario of Bengali's Marxist theatre movement, said of the audience's relationship to the performance:

> They bring their actual life experiences to bear upon the stage. They react to plays from the standpoint of their own personal sufferings and have the strength to alter the values enshrined in performance. The audience is the link between life and theatre. (Dutt, 1982, p. 15)

This sense of an organic relationship, and of theatre as part of a wider nexus of socio-political life, in which culture is embraced as part of a revolutionary project, permeated Belfast Community Theatre's work.

## The Belfast People's Theatre

While Father Wilson's theatrical engagement was more sporadic than Belfast Community Theatre's, it offered an important element in the overall role of theatre within the community, and I would like to offer a brief outline of it here.

This rebel cleric used theatre, he said, as a means of 'affirming the dignity of a nationalist community widely regarded as a ghetto.' (Pilkington, p. 135) Yet, while the Belfast People's Theatre and Belfast Community Theatre were to share both personnel and Conway Mill theatre, their targets and methods were different. A gentle man with a reputation for authorial monomania, Father Wilson's main thrust was satirical. In reviews provocatively entitled, *You're Not Going To Like This,* he dissected with forensic precision the ideological corruption of the social groups he had abandoned - the Roman Catholic hierarchy, the SDLP and the Catholic middle classes. In a letter to this writer, enclosing some of his sketches he wrote:

> Most of the futile, too gentle fury of the enclosed is directed against the church establishment...but by laughing at them we laugh at the whole corrupt boiling of them. Also the ones who march in the streets for South Africa or Guatemala, and reproduce the same conditions at home. (Des Wilson in an undated letter to the author, 1992)

In the *Ecumenical Clergy Song* he parodied this hypocrisy. A row of bishops dance routines to lyrics such as:

> When anyone's rights are in danger
>
> You'll find we will never say Nay
>
> We're always a snip for good causes
>
> As long as they're far, far away.
>
> (Wilson, 1987, You're Not Going To Like This!, play script)

It is hard to measure the impact on West Belfast's Catholic community of sketches such as this, or the *Bishop Interview,* in which the Roman Catholic hierarchy is parodied and mercilessly and brilliantly satirised by one of its own priests.

One of his most striking pieces, *Focailin,* was not a satirical sketch. An expressionistic meditation on obedience and the radical impact of questioning this brief playlet had three characters, Clown, Focailin and Operator. Focailin, suited, clean, urbane, represented institutional authority, the system, the army and judiciary. Clown, a sad faced Grimaldi-like presence, represented the community. Operator was nondescript (in Belfast death comes dressed like my neighbour). The play centres on a series of elliptical conversations between the three. Beckett-like in its tersely allusive language, its dramatic structure is circular (Wilson, 1986, *Focailin,* play script.):

F: You know what has to be done?

O: Kill him.

F: I didn't say that.

O: I said it and you agreed with me.

F: I said nothing. *(Turns to the door.)*

C: What's the price of a revolver?

F: *(Without turning from the door.)* I don't sell revolvers for a job like this.

C: For a job like this, they're free.

O: I said nothing.

F: Then we understand each other.

The dramatic focus is the battle for Operator's lethal allegiance. As such *Focailin* is a call for rational scepticism in the face of authority. Its almost mathematical abstractions are not an evasion of reality, but operate in a Brechtian sense as a formal distanciation: the creation of a needed space for reflection on a traumatic and bloody reality. This is a reality that pressed upon the audience not in abstract, but through the presence of armed soldiers outside the doors of the theatre. When I first heard the piece it was at a rehearsal in a small front room in Andersontown. The performers were from Belfast Community Theatre. Between them these groups offered the community a striking range of radical theatre.

## 1988 'The Rights Of Man' and *Ecce Homo*

In the period following *Sign on the Dotted Line*, the group turned its attention to an issue which, on the surface, could not have been more alien to its community's belief system, or more apparently marginal to the overall nationalist struggle - Gay Liberation. The resulting play, *Ecce Homo*, was to be the group's last, and was never performed. Yet its genesis and development is an important part of this study.

Its history is bound up with the history of both our theatres, and with the politics that shaped our separate but parallel engagements. For Goodchild's activism had precipitated in 1987-8 an important development within the Springhill community when, supported by him, some five young men had 'come out' as gay. This inevitably fed into the group's own politics, as Reid acknowledges:

> We started to look at issues that people wanted to explore within the group...and the gay issue came up...people in the group wanted to highlight the gay issue...and out of that came *Ecce Homo*. *Ecce Homo* was never produced and never will be. And maybe that doesn't matter. (Reid, 1998)

The text began as a series of improvisations, which were taken and written up by Reid. In the same interview, he traced the elements that had led to the script:

> We are in a heavily politicised situation, and it's about rights. How do we treat people inside this politicised situation? Within this 'family'? I have a right within the 'family' to ask those questions. So, how can we on the one hand have the Rights of Man, and yet not seriously consider how we demand those rights? And out of that came *Ecce Homo*. It was also an attempt to highlight what I still regard as the oppressive nature, the insensitive nature, of organised religion. (Reid, 1998)

The story of the drama is straightforward. Emanuel, a young working-class Catholic is planning to move out to share a flat with a young woman, Veronica, and another friend, Simon. Emanuel works on a building site as a labourer. His plans worry his parents. Is Veronica pregnant? Will they be living in sin? As the mother rushes to the priest for advice, and the father reflects that at least his son isn't a 'fruit', Emanuel decides to come out. It is this decision that precipitates the play's actions, as he confronts in turn his mother, his friends, his father, his work mates, and finally, an army patrol which stops him as he is coming out of a gay bar. Only his mother reacts with a confused but unconditional love. For his lover, Simon, the action is not worth the pain. Recognising that he is confined, geographically, ideologically, and militarily, Simon wants to fence off his sexuality: to make it a private space in which he can be free. Emanuel's response to this is as realistic as it is dangerous:

> SIMON: We live in a straight world. We can't change that.
>
> EMANUEL: Aye, straight and narrow. And maybe we can't change it, but we don't have to accept it!

And so the precipitate rush to confront the world begins. The play's last scene takes place on the building site. Emanuel has come out to his work mates, an action triggered by hearing them leer over a page three topless model. As they abuse him, he grabs their copy of *The Sun* newspaper:

> EMANUEL: (*As he speaks he drops crumpled sheets of the newspaper to the floor around him.*) Man: (*reads*) Queer! (*Balls sheet and throws it down.*) Poof! *(Balls*

> *sheet and throws it down.)* Pervert! (*Balls sheet and throws it down.*) Faggot! (*Screws up rest of sheets one by one and throws them down, stops, pauses.*) Faggot. They call me a faggot. I'd like to explain what a faggot is. In the Middle Ages, when they persecuted and burnt witches, the majority of whom were lesbians, they used to collect all the gay men in the village, tie them together, place them at the bottom of the bonfire, and burn them first. That's why they call us...faggots. (*Takes a box of matches from his pocket and steps on to the pile of newspaper.*) Well, I'm gay. I'm a faggot. (*Holds out matches towards audience.*) Who wants to burn me?

The image is taken directly from Theatreworks. It had been created by Goodchild many years earlier, and had been part of our repertoire of sketches. This 'quotation' is part of others in the play, including material from Bertolt Brecht and Nelson Mandela. Reid is forthright about his borrowing from Theatreworks:

> That seemed perfectly logical to me. You don't reinvent the wheel. Here's a man...here's two men who have been through a particular experience...have done theatre...and it works and it has something to say to us. If I like what you say - and that's what I want to say - use it! (Reid, 1998)

These 'quotations' insist on the existence of a movement, of a community of endeavour, that reaches both back and across history. In one of the play's most poetic sections the narrator talks of a 'Freedom Line' which weaves through the world, connecting the sites of suffering and liberation, connecting individuals and collectives, groups and societies, and drawing them into a network.

Where the Freedom Line began or will end, no one knows. It was seen the day that a tired black woman refused to give up her seat to a white oppressor...it was seen and heard on the streets of Derry, Yorkshire and Alabama...

The play was never staged. However cohesive the community's class militancy, issues of gender and sexual rights were always subsidiary to the main aims of the republican movement. Indeed, Adams managed to secure the support of hardliners for his constitutional road in 1986 by dropping references to a woman's 'right to choose' from the party's platform. Internal censorship by the community existed in a symbiotic tension with the censorship of the state apparatus. This was not a matter of prescription in any settled way, but of constant internal negotiation, and was related to the prosecution of the military struggle. While Reid and the group were committed to a liberation strategy, it was work effected from the ground of a critical but unconditional solidarity. Reid:

> This community is not perfect, but I want to be part of the solution to its problems. I'm not going to be, or lend, ammunition to any outside bourgeois, imperialist forces...I'm using clichés I know...but you know what I'm saying. The boot was on our neck. And you had to get people standing up first and starting to push that boot off. And maybe *Ecce Homo* didn't have the same priority. And I hold my hands up, *mea culpa*. But I reckon it was probably one of the best things we've ever put together. (Reid, 1998)

Criticism of nationalists for not foregrounding gay issues during an irredentist war is similar to that aimed at the black consciousness movement for their perceived failure to take on the class dimensions of apartheid. (Steadman, pp. 55-75) It is a complex matter: fractions within the community did, like Belfast Community Theatre, push identity agendas and take risks with them. To those from outside these experiences who criticise activists we may, with justice, ask: What have you done for gay rights in your own state? Or for human rights in Ireland? The British left's response to Section 28 and homophobia in general was marked by pusillanimity and silence.

## A Liberation Struggle Served by Liberation Theatres

By 1990 the groups had ceased to operate in the same regular way. Events on the streets, the development of different imperatives as nationalism moved towards the historic accommodation represented by the Good Friday Agreement of 1997, and the need for members to earn a living - all these impacted on the group's longevity. For Reid, McKnight and the others, theatre had never, in any case, been a profession: it was an intervention, one action among others in the broader struggle. What such theatre offered, besides political commitment, was what Reid called 'the authenticity of the voice.' Form was derived from the desire to give the suppressed nationalist experience shape, a concrete form that, as in *Sign on the Dotted Line*, could nourish hope and strengthen resistance.

Rooted in Irish culture, Belfast Community Theatre's range - the use and reworking of Beckett, the performance of texts by Lady Gregory, Yeats and Brecht, the writing of new plays, the 'Living Newspaper' forms, and so on - demonstrated a breadth of dramatic interest which places it outside the British political theatres of the 1960s and 1970s. To find a comparable concentration of elements, of a coherent, geographical, class based experiment that was, in every sense, catholic and aesthetically adventurous, one would have to turn to Littlewood and MacColl's Theatre Workshop or, more appositely, the Workers' Theatre groups of the 1920s. Belfast Community Theatre and the Peoples Theatre belong to this lineage, a lineage defined by a double project: to educate a community not only through theatre, but also *about* theatre.

And while these theatres emerged from a highly effective indigenous resistance culture, they are also significant for the way their concerns, ideology and processes reflect the concerns and practice of the liberation theatres of the South.[19] For example, Plastow and Tsehaye's essay in *Theatre Matters* on the work of the Eritrean Cultural Brigades during the war of secession with Ethiopia, depicts conditions of production that Reid, McKnight, and Des Wilson would recognise. They describe a practice defined by the immanence of death, by a pragmatic attitude to forms, by a collective and deeply political construction of texts, and by the political relationship between performer and activist. (Tsehaye with Plastow, 1998, pp. 36-54) African theatre offers other resonances. John S. Mbiti has stressed the relationship between the African worldview and theatre processes as one in which 'whatever happens to the individual happens to the whole group, and whatever happens to the whole group happens to the individual'. (Chinyowa, 2000, pp. 87-96) The radical Kenyan writer and educationalist, Ngugi wa Thiong'o, talks of African theatre, as 'an activity among other activities' which, offering both entertainment and instruction, was 'a strict matter of life and death, and of communal survival'. 'Theatre is not a building,' he wrote, 'People make theatre. Their life is the very stuff of drama.' (Thiong'o, pp. 238-244) The Dunlop Players, a worker theatre from Durban, South Africa, wrote of their work that 'it educates people about our struggle and puts across a true picture of things - our picture.' For the Dunlop workers 'the fundamental element common to all the plays is the identity of creators and audiences as members of the working class and its struggles.' They iterate the practical difficulty of making theatre within a life defined by struggle:

> despite all the enthusiasm, energy and the belief in the importance of their work, there are times when the obstacles, difficulties and problems facing creative workers seems insurmountable. (Von Kotze, 1987, pp. 83-92)

These are sentiments with which Belfast Community Theatre and Belfast People's Theatre would absolutely identify. The emphasis on the interplay of collective and individual, and of the relation of theatre to fundamental issues of political survival, human rights, and national identity, places the two theatres firmly within the global liberation theatre movement.

Indeed, what is interesting is the extent to which Belfast Community Theatre and the People's Theatre occupied a transitional ground between twentieth century Western European political theatre models on the one hand, and the Freirean, process-based and liberation practices of the South on the other. Nor was their work unique: to their achievement we may conjoin that of other theatres from the north of Ireland in the period. Derry Frontline, a group which evolved from Manchester Frontline and which was based upon a systematic application of Freirean methodology has been a significant group. (Pilkington, 1994, pp. 17-45) Other groups included Charabanc, Dubbeljoint, Just Us women's theatre, Ardoyne Youth Theatre, the H Block theatres, and the Derry 'Whitehouse' workshops. All these were, or are, part of a nexus of radical theatre activity. They belong to the global network of liberation theatres that includes the work of Asian, African and Latin American liberation groups.[20]

For Reid and Belfast Community Theatre, theatre was neither text or building, method or profession, but a social practice and a political weapon of great power and beauty:

> I could reach into it tomorrow, pick it up again. It's not the be all and end all. But to me it comes close to being the be all and end all as a means to expression, as a means of empowerment. And there was a philosophy at work there...we met people...yourself, people from England, Scotland, from all over the world...so it wasn't a theatre hammered out of insularity. It was a theatre hammered out of an awareness that the plastic bullet that was fired here today could be fired in Sheffield in the morning.

Could be fired in Scotland next year. That the judicial tactics that they used here could be used in Sheffield in the morning... And so Belfast Community Theatre was a moment...was an experience. It's still alive because it's alive in everybody who was involved in creating it. And so until I die, it lives, until Marie dies, it lives. (Reid, 1998)

## Notes

1. I will use the nationalist's designation in preference to the state's term of 'Northern Ireland'.

2. While the first IRA ceasefire was in August 1994, they resumed hostilities in February 1996 with the Canary Wharf bombing. It was not until July 1997 that the present ceasefire began.

3. Formed in 1919, the Irish Republican Army (Oglaigh n hEireannn), has fought ever since for a 32 county, united Ireland. It is the armed wing of Sinn Fein (Ourselves Alone). In 1970, the organisation split into Official and Provisional sections. The latter, known as the Provisionals prosecuted a military struggle between 1970 and 1994. The Official IRA split again in 1975, with the majority forming the Workers Party, a neo-Marxist group.

4. For a powerful account of the early phase of the conflict see: Eamonn McCann (1980), *War in an Irish Town*.

5. From an interview given by Belfast Community Theatre to the author, Belfast, 1986.

6. The house was demolished in 1988, as part of a rebuilding programme. The new Springhill House is located nearby at 6-7 Springhill Close.

7. See for example, Paulo Freire (1972), *Pedagogy of the Oppressed*; (1972), *Cultural Action for Freedom*; and Clodovis Boff (1981), 'The Nature of Basic Christian Communities'.

8. For a detailed, bullet-by-bullet account of Ballymurphy in the first years of the conflict see: Ciaron De Baroid (1985), *Ballymurphy at War*.

9. The Hunger Strike was the endgame of the 'Dirty Protest' that had begun in 1976 in response to the removal of political status from republican prisoners. The charismatic Bobby Sands was the first to die on 5 April 1981. Nine more prisoners died before relatives ended the protest in October.

10. Sands became MP for Fermanagh/South Tyrone on 9 April 1981 in a by-election. Following his death his election agent, Owen Carroll, was elected to replace him.

11. From an interview given by Joe Reid to the author, Belfast, 1998.

12. The echo of William's structure of feeling is acknowledged. What I wish to point to is the tendency for structures of human experience – the brutalisation of daily life, suspension of civil liberties, harassment, a militarised judiciary, torture, poverty, communal strife – to throw up repetitions and echoes in the social values, forms of communal association, and theatre used by

oppositional forces and by oppressed groups. These structures are not particular to any system, but are found in democracies and totalitarian states, in oligarchies and quasi-feudal societies.

13. Named after their cellular layout, the H Blocks were the main holding prison in the north of Ireland for both republican and loyalist prisoners.

14. He notes that Paulo Freire's *Pedagogy of the Oppressed* was a key text for republicans. It was Freire's support of Boal that convinced the prisoners to try Forum Theatre methodologies.

15. The Emancipation Act had removed bars to Catholic participation in Parliament, the judiciary and the civil service, but at the cost of raising the property qualification for voting, thus disenfranchising the Catholic poor.

16. Active in the 1840s, Young Ireland was formed by radical intellectuals, and was influenced by the pan European nationalist movements of the period. The group launched an unsuccessful rising in 1848.

17. A useful account of the critical early period in the peace process can be found in Eamonn Mallie and David McKittrick (1996), *The Fight for Peace – the Secret Story Behind the Irish Peace Process*, London: Heinemann. Their latest work (2001), *Endgame in Ireland*, London: Hodder and Stoughton, offers a fascinating insight into the making of the Good Friday Agreement, and details developments up to August 2001.

18. On Sunday 6 March 1988, three unarmed Irish Republican Army members, including Maraid Farrell, were shot dead by undercover members of the Special Air Service (SAS) in Gibraltar. The episode sparked intense controversy and began a chain of events that lead to a series of deaths in Northern Ireland on 16 March 1988 and 19 March 1988.

19. The term now used in place of the pejorative 'developing world' to refer to Latin America, Africa and South East Asia. The corresponding term for Western Europe and the USA is the North.

20. For an excellent account of the group, and of their relationship to Dubbeljoint see: Helen Lojek (1999), 'Playing Politics with Belfast's Charabanc Theatre Company,' in *Politics and Performance in Contemporary Northern Ireland*, p. 83. Also Maria DiCenzo (1993), 'Charabanc Theatre Company: Placing Women Centre Stage in Northern Ireland,' *Theatre Journal*, 45: 2, pp. 175-184.

## References

Adams, Gerry (1986), *The Politics of Irish Freedom,* Dingle, Co. Kerry: Brandon Books.

Adams, Gerry (1996), *Before the Dawn, an Autobiography*, Dublin: Brandon Press.

Ashley, Jane *et al* (1985), *Breaking the Nation, a guide to Thatcher's Britain,* London: Pluto Press.

Baroid, Ciaron de (1985), *Ballymurphy at War*, Belfast: Springhill Press.

Boff, Clodovis (1981), 'The Nature of Basic Christian Communities', *Conciliana Magazine*, no. 144.

Chinyowa, Kennedy C. (2000), 'More Than Mere Story-Telling: the pedagogical significance of African ritual Theatre,' *Studies in Theatre and Performance*, 20: 2.

Curtis, Liz (1984), *Ireland - the Propaganda War*, London: Pluto.

DiCenzo, Maria (1993), 'Charabanc Theatre Company: Placing Women Centre Stage in Northern Ireland,' *Theatre Journal*, 45: 2, pp. 175-184.

Dutt, Uptal (1982), *Towards a Revolutionary Theatre*, Calcutta: Sarkar.

Freire, Paulo (1972), *Pedagogy of the Oppressed,* (trans. by Myra Bergman Ramos) Harmondsworth: Penguin.

Freire, Paulo (1972), *Cultural Action for Freedom,* (trans. by Myra Bergman Ramos) Harmondsworth: Penguin.

Kelley, Kevin (1982), *The Longest War - Northern Ireland and the IRA*, Co. Kerry: Brandon Books.

Kotze, Astrid Von (1987), 'Workers' Theatre in South Africa', *New Left Review*, no. 163, May-June.

Lojek, Helen (1999), 'Playing Politics with Belfast's Charabanc Theatre Company,' in John P. Harrington and Elizabeth J. Mitchell (eds.) *Politics and Performance in Contemporary Northern Ireland*, Amherst: University of Massachusetts Press.

Magill, Tom (1998), 'Theatre as Democracy', *Fortnight Magazine*, November.

Mallie, Eamonn and McKittrick, David (1996), *The Fight for Peace - the Secret Story Behind the Irish Peace Process*, London: Heinemann.

Mallie, Eamonn and McKittrick, David (2001), *Endgame in Ireland*, London: Hodder and Stoughton.

McCann, Eamonn (1980), *War in an Irish Town*, London: Pluto.

Ngugi wa Thiong'o, 'The Language of African Theatre', in Jan Cohen-Cruz (ed.) *Radical Street Performance,* London: Routledge, pp. 238-244.

O'Callaghan, Sean (1999), *The Informer*, London: Corgi.

Lionel Pilkington (1994), 'From Resistance to Liberation with Derry Frontline: an interview with Dan Baron Cohen', *Drama Review*, 38: 4.

Pilkington, Lionel (1994), 'Theatre and Insurgency in Ireland', *Essays in Theatre / Etudes Theatrales* , 12: 2.

Schama, Simon (2000), *A History of Britain: At the Edge of the World?* London: BBC Worldwide Ltd.

Steadman, Ian, 'Race Matters in South African Theatre', in Boon and Plastow (eds.) *Theatre Matters*.

Stevenson Jonathan (1996), *We Wrecked the Place - Contemplating an End to the Northern Irish Troubles*, New York: Simon and Schuster.

Tsehaye, Solomon with Plastow, Jane (1998), 'Making Theatre for a Change: two plays of the Eritrean Liberation Struggle', in Richard Boon and Jane Plastow, (eds,) *Theatre Matters: Performance and Culture on the World Stage*, Cambridge: Cambridge University Press.

Toolis, Kevin (1995), *Rebel Hearts*, London: Picador.

Willett, J. (1986) (ed. and trans.), *Brecht on Theatre: the Development of an Aesthetic*, London: Methuen.

# Crossing Boundaries and Struggling for Language: Using Drama with Women as a Means of Addressing Psycho-social-cultural Issues in a Multi-cultural Context in Contemporary Copenhagen

*Carole Angela Christensen*

As the title implies, the following narrative is about women who are crossing many boundaries, both physically in leaving their own countries of origin, and also culturally and psychologically in their attempts to come to terms with living in a society foreign to them. In this essay I describe and assess the use of drama with immigrant and refugee women suffering from psychological trauma and stress symptoms, where learning ability is inhibited. While working towards such goals as language acquisition, and an increase in self-esteem and well-being, an attempt was to be made to establish an attitudinal perspective towards the traumas that had taken control of their lives. It was hoped that such a renewed awareness would effect an improvement in their quality of life.

Due to linguistic barriers, a methodology was devised for communication between myself as drama facilitator, the assisting teachers, and the participants. Efforts were made to create a safe and secure environment so that learning and development could take place. It was also hoped that this approach would facilitate the participants bringing their personal experiences into the work. Interpreters were used regularly to ensure that important information regarding practical details and participant response was conveyed correctly. Although participants did not choose to review any deeper problematic aspects of their lives, the project was considered successful due to considerable linguistic improvement and noticeable signs of positive personal development in many of the participants.

## Background Context

On the basis of my previous work as a drama worker with immigrants and refugees, I was approached by *Etnisk Radgivningcenter Noor* (a counselling centre for ethnic minorities in Copenhagen) to try a new teaching approach with a group of women from the ethnic minorities living within Copenhagen. A major reason for initiating this project was the awareness that spoken language develops best through conversation and communication outside of the classroom, with individuals other than the teacher. Educational - therapeutic - drama was to be the proposed method. Ideas that informed this approach were those of the American psychologist, Howard Gardner, whose research and writings propose that human beings possess seven different kinds of intelligence. As much conventional teaching is based mainly on linguistic intelligence, those individuals whose learning potential lies in other areas (e.g. musical, rhythmic, logical, kinaesthetic etc.) are at a disadvantage. As Educational Drama and Theatre encompasses a whole range of activities that utilise the multiple intelligences and stimulate such human faculties as movement, speech, imagination and sensory awareness, a more comprehensive developmental learning process is possible.

Gardner also proposes that genuine acquisition of knowledge is a process where not only factual knowledge is acquired, but also where understanding takes place. In this important respect, drama conventions provide opportunities for different aspects of life to be explored in a fictionalised context. Through this process, participants have the opportunity to take on other identities within that fictionalised context, facilitating not only a deeper understanding of the corresponding actual situation, but also encourage a more free and fluent use of the new language.

## Description of Centre and Clients

The Counselling Centre, as well as being staffed by a multicultural team of psychologists, social and educational workers and relaxation therapists, contains a small school where tuition in Danish as a second language is offered. This is part of a stratagem for building up self-esteem and providing a secure 'oasis' of stability on a daily basis. The school is organised in very small single gender groups, catering for all levels of literacy. The intake of clients is continual and teachers can expect new arrivals from week to week. The period of time during which clients attend the school varies, depending on individual needs. Transfers to normal language centres or occupational centres are motivated by improvement of the wider condition of clients and not on language proficiency alone.

The seventeen women in question with whom I worked were between the ages of 25 and 50. They came from a diverse range of countries in continents ranging from Africa, the Far East and the Middle East. They had all been in Denmark for between two and fourteen years and had attended the school for varying periods - two weeks to well over a year. The educational and social background of the participants varied greatly, ranging from illiteracy to those with university degrees. A few had, beside their own language, previous knowledge of French or English, with differing degrees of fluency. The majority had children and were married, some were separated/divorced, and one was widowed. Although few of them had working experience, a couple had professional skills and some had held responsible positions in their own countries. They were using the centre's services for a variety of reasons: post-traumatic stress disorder, physical disability, psycho-social (family) problems and mental disorders.

Attendance frequency, I was forewarned, could be expected to vary. Some participants could be relied upon to attend classes regularly and punctually, whilst others would turn up sporadically, an occurrence owing more to their state of mind and emotional well-being or family issues, rather than an unwillingness to attend.

## Goals and Background to the Project

The goals of the project were divided into two levels:

1. The primary *Visible* goal - to use educational drama techniques to improve the participant's knowledge of the Danish language and promote wider emotional well-being and self-esteem.

2. The secondary *Invisible* goal - this was far more venturesome. I had previously used drama in language training also as a means to clarify and extend understanding of personal and cultural issues within multi cultural groups. The staff at *Noor* thought that by giving the clients the opportunity to create dramatisations of significant or traumatic events in their lives, those participants would be able to create a 'distance' between themselves and those events. It was hoped that, if this were achievable, those individuals would gain the motivation and means to cope with life demands and function more creatively and positively within their new country and culture.

This secondary motivational goal was inspired by the research of Bessel A Van der Kolk, who points to the importance for trauma victims to find a language to express and communicate their experiences without reliving at a deep emotional level the horror of their experiences. Improvement and healing can be brought about by helping the victim to understand that:

• 'Remembering trauma is not equivalent to experiencing it again'.

• 'Those traumas had a beginning, middle and end and that the event now belongs to one's personal history'.

In dramatic terms this can also be explained by what Augusto Boal terms *metaxis*. *Metaxis* occurs when an artistic representation of reality is created and shown in the aesthetic space - the stage - and is experienced in two ways simultaneously. The meta-reality of the play occurring at the same time within the 'here and now' of the real world. The incident therefore becomes part of both worlds at the same time.

The staff and myself tentatively reasoned that if the women, embedded in a safe, caring and secure environment, were able to reproduce dramatised representations of the traumatic incidents in their lives and experience/observe them from a new vantage point; it could be a milestone on the way to recovery. Although none of the *teaching* staff involved were trained therapists, it was felt that the close inter-woven support of all staff and clients at the centre would help support this delicate, therapeutic process.

## Structure and Time Scale

Although the participants were accustomed to meeting each other during the daily coffee break, the teachers prepared for the project by bringing the three classes involved together for musical activities. This was done for several consecutive weeks to get them used to being together in a larger group. The actual project would start with an introductory meeting where participants, interpreters, class teachers and myself as the drama facilitator would all be involved. The project was to run over a period of seven weeks, the half-term holiday occurring after the fourth week making a useful halfway mark. At the last session before the holiday interpreters would again be able to make an evaluative feedback. The sixth week would follow the same pattern as before, whereas work in the seventh week was scheduled on all four days. The project would end with an event where the women would have the opportunity of inviting friends, interpreters, case workers and others to see some of their work, followed by a final evaluation.

## Practical Considerations and Pre-conditions

In order to avoid causing unnecessary disruption and anxiety for the clients involved, it was decided that the project would be carried out at the centre's premises, even though the rooms were very small and not really conducive to drama. However, the clients' routines were to be disrupted as little as possible. After some negotiation, a larger room was made available one morning a week, and every day during the final week. The restrictions imposed on the activities that were carried out in the small classroom, contrasting with the movement-based exercises and games that the larger space permitted, enabled a secure routine to develop. In the small room at the beginning of the week, after the separation of the weekend, intimacy was renewed and reinforced, and confidence gained for the women to extend themselves two days later in the larger space.

## Teachers' Participation

At our final meeting before the drama sessions commenced, the three participating teachers and myself drew up guidelines as to what our respective roles would be and how various tasks would be divided. As visiting drama facilitator, I would prepare and plan the sessions and activities. I would give the teachers instructions in advance as to words, terms and phrases that I planned to use in the coming session, so that they could introduce them to the classes beforehand (for example, 'form a circle', 'work in pairs' and 'change partners'). During the sessions the teachers would, if necessary, rephrase my explanations to reinforce understanding, or repeat them perhaps in English. New words were also reinforced by a teacher writing them on the board and later distributing them to other teachers with whom the clients would have contact.

The teachers would take an active part in all activities, apart from those in which the participants were specifically encouraged to communicate to generate their own themes and decisions. On these occasions the participants worked in small groups without depending on the teacher to take the lead. The teachers would also assist in helping to demonstrate what was required at given moments. The clients were used to placing considerable store upon the example and guidance of the teacher as role model and so the staff were able to help lead and initiate through this.

Immediately after each session we would briefly evaluate the day's events and I would, if possible, advise the teachers as to any words they should present to the women before my next visit.

## The Introductory Session

The purpose of the introductory session was to create a secure and 'optimistic' attitude to the project by providing information, both in words and actions, and to enable the clients to voice queries and anxieties about the forthcoming events. Surprisingly, the atmosphere was much less tense than expected. Emphasis was placed upon the assertion that by playing games, using the whole of one's being - not just the mind - made for easier learning. To help reduce tension and raise a smile, the team also proposed that the activities were renowned for inducing relaxation and laughter, which in turn increased blood-circulation and improved the complexion! These statements provoked an emotional response from the most senior woman in the group:

> 'How can you expect us to laugh when we, unhappy and anxious...have lain awake all night?'

To this I replied very seriously that I couldn't give guarantees for personal happiness but assured her that I knew and was profoundly sympathetic to their difficulties, and would naturally respect and accept whatever responses arose from the work. This reply was quietly digested. She wiped her eyes and we continued with the session. I emphasised also that it was better for them to come to school and watch, yet still be part of the proceedings, rather than to stay at home if they felt uneasy with the drama work. No one would press them to join in any activity that they felt uncomfortable about.

Some simple games and exercises were initiated. A simple presentation exercise involving a soft, cloth-covered ball as a focus point, together with the simple question-and-answer phrases: 'What is your name?', 'Where do you come from?', 'My name is X', 'I come from Y' - the ball thrown back and forth across the circle with each response. This was followed by a laughter-provoking 'Changing Places' game, involving all persons present and providing a welcome release in tension. That everyone, staff included, displayed the same eagerness to grab any available chair created a bond of togetherness and equality between all those present.

From this auspicious position an imagination exercise was introduced where a ruler was used to represent all manner of objects. The purpose of this activity was partly to introduce the new direction that their education was taking and also to create an awareness that this new direction would accentuate other qualities and skills than was usual in the classroom. The game provided the same starting point to all present, those with fluency in Danish and those without, the literate and illiterate. As often happens in this kind of work, those personalities with highly developed and rather rigid intellectual and logical skills, experienced difficulty. I clearly indicated that the ruler could be passed on if anyone lacked ideas. There was no pressure in any way to participate in the exercise. Personal boundaries and limitations were respected. Two of the older women who were weary and declined to participate in one or more of the activities joined in through the use of the ruler. One of them, using the ruler as a prop, showed a folk dance from her culture with such gusto that everyone started clapping to the beat. During this session, the teachers emphasised and reinforced the new verbal phrases and expressions used, with the two hour session finishing upon a very positive note.

## Framework and Activities

I decided to establish a regular routine for the work with some parallels to the usual classroom routine so as to provide a secure and predictable framework into which more challenging themes and activities could be drawn. The morning started with everyone seated on chairs in a circle where general phrases relating to social greetings and enquiries about personal welfare were practised. The dimensions and shape for this opening varied as time went by and grew more varied. As enthusiasm and confidence for the main activities grew, so the need for a safe introduction slowly diminished. A quiet physical warm up exercise followed by a fast moving game was then introduced.

As is generally known and recognised in the field of drama pedagogy, the benefits of any given exercise or activity can span over a wealth of diverse focal points. For example, a fast moving game of 'Tag' with 'Home' (i.e. holding another person's hands or giving them a hug) can facilitate trust, co-operation, and most importantly in the context under discussion, a cheerful and optimistic atmosphere in which anxieties and withdrawal are less likely to be induced. Daniel Coleman, writing of *emotional intelligence* shows how laughter and lively well-being causes people to think more creatively. He describes how emotions have typical physiological responses, the bodily reaction to this condition of happiness being:

> An increased activity in a brain centre that inhibits negative feelings and fosters an increase in available energy and a quieting of those that generate worrisome thought. But there is no particular shift in physiology save a quiescence, which makes the body recover more quickly from the biological arousal of upsetting emotions. This configuration offers the body a general rest, as well as readiness and enthusiasm for whatever task is at hand.

If the task is learning new language, a cheerful relaxed mood brought about by playing one of the simple games described above can then create fertile conditions for the acquisition of that knowledge. In this way, 'Person to Person', an exercise devised by Augusto Boal to extend bodily awareness, while creating relaxation and enjoyment, proved to be an excellent way to practice anatomical vocabulary, whilst also encouraging co-operation and imaginative thinking.

The energetic physical game led into simple stretching exercises to release muscular tension and reduce stiffness, beneficial at not only body-level but also activating frames of mind and mood. Swedish Forum Play practitioner, Katrin Byres-Hagen writes, 'to take an unusual physical position is not only a physical experience but also a psychological one, of new thoughts and feelings.'

A short warm-up followed with exercises based on articulating the numerous and very complex Danish vowel sounds. (There are about fifteen of them, compared to three in Urdu and four in Arabic.) This section was followed by one or more 'leading in' activities involving the senses, mime, object/props, and statues. Sessions always finished with relaxing music. It was considered vital that sessions ended with quiet closure enabling thoughts and feelings from the drama session to settle and embed before the clients returned to their daily concerns. Before disbanding, we asked the participants to tell us something about how *they felt* about the drama activities. At this stage, the replies were generally positive but undeveloped: 'It was good fun, nice, fine'.

## Methodology: Communication through Demonstration

The client's limited understanding of Danish language governed to a great extent the activity chosen. For example, a seemingly simple game suddenly becomes extraordinarily complicated when met with repeated expressions of puzzled amazement: 'Are they trying to make fools of us?'

Instructions would often have to be given to the whole group in Danish, then reinforced in English for two Afghani and Iraqi women, who would then translate what they had understood to the clients that they shared common languages with. Inevitably this sequence could and did give rise to misunderstandings. To avoid this time consuming process, I devised a methodology of simplification and exemplification avoiding abstract instructions as much as possible - with inevitable restrictions upon the choice of drama activities.

The chain of instruction was thus:

- Instructions were given verbally, in simple terms, for the most elementary part of the exercise.

- The teachers then carried out the activity with either another member of staff, or, if suitable, by involving a client. In my previous experience of using drama work with clients from authoritarian educational backgrounds, I had seen a strong tendency towards direct reproduction of teachers' examples. It was important for us to counteract this tendency and to communicate an ethos of diversity and encourage inventiveness.

• The instructions were repeated and a short time was allowed for exchange between clients to clarify instructions.

• The activity was begun. If there was still confusion, new attempts were made to activate the process, often using practical demonstration.

• When the first part of the game or activity was functioning smoothly, the next development was introduced.

An exercise for building vocabulary, training memory and observation and encouraging inventiveness was introduced in this manner:

• I sat in a position where everyone could clearly see me and I asked the clients to look at me very carefully for 60 seconds. I then told them to close their eyes or cover them with their hands. I then quickly altered some of the details of my clothing and my posture: rolled up a sleeve, put my shoes on the opposite feet, removed an earring, changed my facial expression, and thrust out my leg in front of me. The clients were told to open their eyes and recount the changes that they noticed.

• The next step was for two teachers to sit opposite each other and take it in turn to make six changes in their appearance and then observe and describe the changes.

• Thirdly, the clients were instructed to find a partner and do likewise. The teachers then asked them to rearrange their chairs so that they sat opposite each other. At this point, some confusion arose. The clients did not get down to the activity but waited. This then provided an excellent opportunity to teach the concept of 'everyone works at the same time', and so, with the combined efforts of the teacher and myself, we helped each couple get started. In this way everyone was soon working simultaneously and a new term and concept was introduced.

Afterwards, when we had assembled the new words and expressions on the board, this exercise was extended. Again, while the class sat with their eyes closed, the teachers formed a tableau of a 'Family Photograph' depicting a family outing. The same procedure was then followed again successfully.

## Dramatisation and Role Play

Just about everyone in the world today who has access to electronically mediated entertainment and the world of popular film and the soap-opera, has some concept of theatre, even if they have never been inside a theatre building or witnessed a street performance. There was therefore, significantly, no difficulty for the women clients to acknowledge that theatre involves people telling a story by pretending to be someone else.

On the very first day of the project we were able to establish that theatre 'showing stories' was to be a focal point of our work, by improvising a simple story inspired by a few objects that had been used in the previous sensory exercise. I improvised a very short scene from some simple objects, including a pencil and bus ticket, to demonstrate how easily a story could be devised and presented.

The teachers and myself, showing an exemplification of a related situation, often introduced dramatisations and role-plays. I differentiate between dramatisations and role-plays in the following way:

By dramatisation I mean the focal point of the exercise to be the actual situation, whereas in role-play the portrayal and investigation of the persona's occupation, vocabulary and actions is the central focus point. In the former, the task has a more open-ended framework, which gives the participants ample opportunity to bring in their own personal material if they so wish. For example 'Show us something that happened to you during your weekend'. Or, 'One of you is a doctor, the other is ill and goes to the doctor. Decide who might play the various parts in this situation, including a receptionist, and work on this scene'.

Direct verbal improvisation was introduced by using the teacher - in-role technique and the universally familiar theme of shopping - the interaction between buyer and shopkeeper gave even the shyest member of the group the opportunity to participate actively. After describing the shop and surroundings, I left the room and reappeared as an elderly, very familiar, talkative shopkeeper who questioned their choice of purchases, enlisted their help to move the goods, as frightened by a robber, had a subsequent 'bad turn' and had to be taken to hospital. The drama was interrupted every so often to discuss the characters of both customers and shopkeeper. The clients understood the concepts of both personality and characteristics and although strong characterisations sometimes occurred spontaneously in subsequent improvisations, the effort of carrying out dramatisations in a new language was too demanding to expect consistency. The abstract terms of *character* and *role* were not used at the beginning of this work. Other places used in this approach included a hairdressers, a café, a park and kite flying - with the park including a spontaneous act of picking flowers and running away!

There was significant evidence that the *visible* goal of developing communication skills was being achieved. The new language was being constantly used and extended with the clients clearly gaining in confidence and obviously enjoying pleasure observing and commenting upon the various tasks.

One observation about the communication in small task groups: In the beginning, to encourage them as much as possible to produce a 'result' and have the satisfaction of having succeeded, we let the participants form small task groups. The tendency was naturally for them to be together with those of a common language - although this was never an option for the solitary nationals from China, Vietnam and Togo. This soon proved to be a limitation, however, as plans became so elaborate and clients became frustrated by their limited language skills in Danish. After the holiday, however, we made some innovations to extend the use of Danish in group work.

## Progress and Process

After the second session, it became clear to me that to enable the classes to run more smoothly, the teachers needed to have prior knowledge of the day's activities. Knowing in advance what a game or exercise entailed and also their part in it, the teachers would be more able to guide the clients into action. We then started to meet for a fifteen-minute briefing before each session commenced - a tactic that quickly produced the desired effect. The teachers' apprehension that the clients would become less willing to participate in the activities, or to attend school less frequently, proved, happily, to be unfounded. A couple of the clients with very little Danish expressed dissatisfaction and requested traditional lessons with pen, paper and grammar, but the drama was well received by the majority, regardless of their previous educational achievements or trauma related problems with memory. Whereas energy levels fluctuated greatly from one day to the next, the speed with which we could introduce different activities and themes for dramatisation was rapid, owing to the willing attitude of the regular attendees. Generally the clients went whole-heartedly into the work and enjoyed it. The participant whose spirit was often dulled by medication, and another exhausted by anxiety-filled nights, surprised us with their efforts and revealed unexpected qualities.

## Personal Breakthroughs

The two participant/clients who the teachers felt had made the most breakthroughs during the drama project were Sadia and Kym.

In the earlier part of the project I had noticed that Sadia, a younger, withdrawn, childless woman from Iraq, undergoing treatment for severe depression, would participate in the warming up games and exercises, but at some point leave the room. Appearing in the staff room at break, she would tell us that she wasn't well, or had a headache and was going home. In one exercise we worked in groups of four or five with a teacher presiding in each. She was sitting beside me, and just before it was her turn, I suddenly noticed that her chair was empty. As this pattern became apparent, we were unsure as to the reason. Could this really be a health issue or perhaps religious or cultural? Her teacher asked her privately if she was distressed by the drama work, but her response was non-committal. This pattern continued and Sadia was rarely completely absent. We reasoned that it was best to accept her attendance pattern without further comment for the time being. After the holiday we noticed a decided change and Sadia's participation in activities increased. That she refused to carry out an action where she would be the focus of attention was a wonderful advancement. She had become confident enough to indicate what she would or would not do, rather than just discretely leaving the room. She also took a small but active part in the final week's work. Staff at the centre generally felt that the drama project had been a significant turning point for Sadia, who showed herself to be far more cheerful and open in the months that followed. Had her experience of the drama project facilitated this change in her well-being and demeanour?

Endemic for persons from South East Asia is a greater difficulty with Danish pronunciation than other ethnic groups. Kym, a shy, timid Vietnamese woman, had a congenital deformity of the jaw that made pronunciation of Danish an even more difficult task. Her teacher mentioned that in class she would sometimes become very frustrated by the difficulties she was experiencing and become blocked. At the introductory meeting she excused herself for being old (36 years!) and often wasn't able to understand the proceedings. Her fears were ungrounded. Kym not only understood, but also proved to be a regular and very active participant, eagerly taking initiative and constantly surprising us all. Not only did she become more talkative, her speech was much more clear and certain and her vocabulary more extensive.

The extraordinary progress of these two women does seem splendid, but one can speculate as to the reasons. Had these more confident, assertive personalities always been present within them? Quite probably the linguistic restrictions governing their lives in Denmark, together with other traumatic experiences related to their own country's political circumstances, defined their sense of personal dysfunction and profound unhappiness. Had the drama affected not only a return to their previous, more certain, sense of themselves, or even facilitated a new direction of hope and self-expression for these women? This we will probably never know.

## The Project - Midway

At this point in time the teachers had already noticed some positive effects that the drama sessions had brought about, both in relation to individuals and to the group as a whole. Participants were less shy about using the language, some seemed generally more cheerful, and there was an atmosphere of trust and fellowship in the group.

The planned evaluation with interpreters was to enable the participants to voice their opinions about the project without being hindered by a deficit of language. Although we had drawn conclusions on the basis of what we had seen and experienced, we felt that it was equally - if not more - important to find out what was actually going on in their minds. Were there issues that they were too polite to mention, or feared to tell us, because of adverse experiences in authoritarian education systems?

When the class was assembled with the interpreters, I told the participants that it was important for me (and the teachers) to know how they had experienced the sessions. We needed to know so that we could make improvements where necessary.

This was welcomed and taken very seriously and they were eager to give their views. For many, it was an act of achievement to speak in front of a large gathering and be listened to attentively. There was a general consensus that the drama activities were beneficial: the physical activities were very worthwhile and they were learning and using more Danish than ever before:

- 'We learn better when we are having fun'.

- 'It's good to be forced to speak Danish...I have put aside my shyness'.

- 'I learn when I'm here at school, but forget when I get home, so it's very good for me to practice in this way'.

- 'It's good to have the opportunity to use Danish more than usual, although it's sometimes difficult to carry on conversations and carry out the tasks'.

- 'It was tiring at first and not much fun, but soon I started enjoying it'.

- 'Miming is good - one doesn't need to speak'.

Several of the participants requested very directly that we work with daily life situations: visiting the doctor, conversations with nursery staff, parent-teacher meetings and so on.

In my response to these remarks I acknowledged that they had been given some rather large challenges, and thanked them for taking the tasks seriously and doing their best. I agreed that mime required les effort but did not give sufficient opportunity for language activity. I thanked them for their confidence and trust, and the warmth they had shown towards me. I would take note of their suggestions and requests when planning for future sessions.

## Continuation and Conclusion

Again, the constellation in the class changed after the holiday. Attendance for a few of the participants who had formerly been dependable now became haphazard. Yet others, of whom we had seen so little, appeared more frequently and Sadia became more active. As many of the participants had expressed the wish for certain life event-related themes, my strategy after the holiday was to provide drama activities in that context. We now concentrated on the themes of healthcare and parenting, using a combination of teacher-in-role techniques to encourage active involvement, and group tasks for independent work preparing role-plays in given themes and contexts. It was very clear in the ensuing work that the participants were bringing in a wealth of knowledge and experience, and that those who had lived here for many years surprised themselves by discovering that they owned a considerable passive vocabulary.

We now introduced a new element into the work by insisting on multi-language task groups to encourage further conversation in Danish. There were some protests to this innovation. We explained that we were now giving them enhanced opportunities to actively practice what they had learnt, that this was still a learning experience where they weren't expected to be 'perfect', but had the opportunity to experiment and practice. This was accepted.

We presented the class with a framework for a simultaneous role-play in the casualty department in a hospital; with the teachers in role as receptionist, nurse and doctors. The atmosphere of trust that had been built up during the previous weeks was very evident in the work that followed. The 'patients' explicitly paraded their maladies, groaning, fainting and becoming violently sick. It became clear that many did already have an active - if limited - vocabulary to deal with the situation (nouns and verbs) and that a wealth of new vocabulary relating to anatomy and symptoms was being evoked. One disturbing fact that came to light through this role-play was that many of the women had very little knowledge of basic anatomy.

Next, the teachers costumed themselves in an exaggerated manner as typical Danish parents and a schoolteacher, presenting two very recognisable situations involving the conflicting opinions of both parents and teacher. An issue of contention in the Muslim community - attendance at school camps - was also brought into one of the scenes and later discussed by the whole class. In the presentations that followed, the participants surprised us greatly by showing a freer and extended use of language when in the context of a role-play supported by costume and simple props. Perhaps the following elements contributed to this positive development:

• The costuming caused a deeper identification with the taken role or simply signifies a release from the confines of the self.

• There was a specific importance and relevance of the social conflict situations enacted.

• The context of 'parenting' roles and situations motivated a stronger need for self-confidence and competence.

## The Final Week

As we reached the final week, the plan was as follows:

• Participants were to choose to work with one of the three major themes that held relevance for them: i.e. health care, parent-teacher co-operation and shopping.

• They were to develop a narrative in relation to their chosen theme(s).

• There was to be rehearsal and language practice.

• There was to be a final presentation and evaluation of the project.

Shopping and parent-teacher co-operation were the preferred themes. The educationally based strategy of letting the participants work in autonomous groups to maximise their language practice, and to gain confidence and experience by planning and carrying out tasks independently, was perhaps, in retrospect, adhered to too rigidly on my part. By the second day, three short improvised plays were prepared: two dealt with shopping situations in - respectively - a dress shop and a green grocer's shop, and a third with a parent-teacher consultation.

The action in both of these two plays varied immensely from day to day, depending on which participants were present at the time, the stronger ones being more able to develop conversation and conflict, the weaker ones content to make their purchases and leave. It was at this point, during a rehearsal on the third day, that I felt for the first (and only) time apprehension about a participant's emotional well-being. Sadia - in the role of a bothersome child nagging for chocolate, became frantically excited, crying repeatedly, 'I want chocolate, I want chocolate'. Fearing that she was becoming hysterical, I quickly pretended to be a waiting customer and gave her an object wrapped in paper, which she immediately began to examine, and the play proceeded. In the subsequent repetition during the dress rehearsal, the shopkeeper dealt more quickly with the nagging child and the scene progressed smoothly.

The parent-teacher consultation had a more extended narrative. A teacher is concerned with a certain pupil's progress. The pupil, when approached, tells of problems at home. The teacher telephones the parents to arrange a meeting and discovers that they are now divorced. At the subsequent meeting the husband turns up drunk, and angrily refuses to help his child, preferring life with his Danish girlfriend. The wife and teacher unite to assist the child.

This short play, lasting only about fifteen minutes, was moving but also contained moments of contrasting humour and comedy. The husband, played with great enjoyment by a woman from Afghanistan, was rude and belligerent. The audience loved to see him staggering around - so clearly self-centred and uncaring for his former wife and child. He looked ridiculous and the audience of women felt that the wife was a stoic and would manage well (if not better) without him.

If one looks beyond the linguistic, educational and even entertainment value of the work, elements of these women's real lives undoubtedly began to surface in a visible and therapeutic way. The direct representation of human behaviour, viewed through the distancing effect of humour along with the careful enunciation of newly found vocabulary, was clearly beneficial. The fact that these aspects of their lives had been 'given names' and brought into the open through the drama helped the participants to make sense of their world and cope with the reality around them. Words that the participants had had difficulty in pronouncing and wanted more practice in were emblematic of deeper personal and social needs: 'beer', 'divorced', 'problems'.

The stage was divided from the rest of the room and audience area by some potted plants and a screen was put up at one side to facilitate entrances and exits. To prepare the participants for new faces in the audience, we arranged for two of the interpreters who were unable to be present on the final day of performance to be present at the dress rehearsal.

The next day was fraught with surprises - several of the participants who had performed so well on the dress rehearsal did not arrive, and a few who did appear had only been present sporadically since the holiday. This caused some consternation and there was a certain amount of juggling with roles. Kym indicated very eagerly that she would take on the role of the dress shop manager, whilst a reticent young Chinese woman who had previously not taken a very active role in the work spontaneously put on a scarf to correspond with the Islamic dress of her shopping companion before going on stage.

We had indicated that the performance was an integral part of the learning process, but that they would have some control over who, apart from teachers and interpreters, would be in the audience. There was a general consensus that female members of centre staff, and female relatives/friends could be present. The number was necessarily limited by the space available. About fifteen women, interpreters, centre staff and a couple of relatives were present. The performance was very well received and everyone was greatly impressed by the increased linguistic ability and self-confidence and personal courage shown by participants. After shared refreshments, with the help of interpreters, we evaluated the whole process.

The participants were asked to relate what they had experienced and learnt during the project, and what they had liked and not liked. There was a tremendous eagerness to relate thoughts and feelings about the events of previous weeks. The general consensus was that the combination of physical activities and drama role-play activities had been very beneficial for promoting well-being and increasing their ability to speak Danish. A few of them mentioned that in the beginning that they had not felt comfortable with the games, although now they would like to work again in this way.

- 'The stretching was good. I try to do it at home even though I can't really remember how. It helps me relax and feel better'.

- 'When we played the part with the scarf, everyone laughed, so I laughed too.'

- 'It was good that we didn't read and write or use our books but that we *spoke*!'

- 'I've really enjoyed going to school in this period.'

- 'I have some good memories and have learnt lots of new words and phrases by doing the plays.'

• 'It was interesting, because we didn't realise that we could speak as much Danish as we actually can. A good discovery!'

## Postscript

Six weeks later, the teachers and myself met to evaluate the project and to bring me up to date with the after-effects and consequences of the Drama Project. The general consensus was that the project had been beneficial both for the participants as well as the teachers.

During the whole of the project, the learning process involved the use of imagination, performing actions in specific contexts without the formal pressure to 'learn', but with an emphasis upon 'doing' and 'being'. In this manner, I believe that we were tapping into a natural, intuitive mode of learning that is related to the way in which a child learns its native language and other social skills.

The teachers were very satisfied and felt that that the primary goals for the project had been accomplished. Regarding the secondary goal, evaluating the results is more provisional and ambiguous. We undoubtedly *did* view scenes that communicated small - but significant? - details of more comprehensive traumatic experiences: air travel in fleeing one's own country; intense physical pain in a hospital bed; and family and relationship conflicts and problems. However, those experiences were generally presented without the *obvious* personal pathos and emotional identification associated with personal reportage. Rather, the strong desire to be autonomous in the present prevailed, spurring them to ask to be taught language for managing their ongoing personal and social lives in Danish society.

The dedication and enthusiastic participation of the teachers was a major factor in the success of the project. It was an extraordinarily significant resource and an enormous asset to have three trained teachers assisting, who clearly enjoyed taking part in the work. I was not given a case history for each woman before I started the project. It was enough for me to know that they had severe personal difficulties that could affect their attempts to participate. It was most interesting then, that that although attendance was unstable, when they did attend, everybody's participation was active and wholehearted. It was a great privilege to work with these courageous women and experience the warmth and affection in their relations with each other and towards teachers, their facilitators and us.

This elicits my final closing question to myself. Had drama been the entirely - or singularly - effective channel for these good results being achieved? There were so many other factors: the enthusiastic teachers - so positive towards the project and so concerned for the welfare and well-being of their students; and the women themselves, who allowed themselves to be creatively challenged. These were each crucial elements to the overall success of the project. How significant is the *context* and *environment* in which drama is explored and enacted, to its potentially therapeutic value and impact?

# Taking Liberties

*Gunduz Kalic*

## Introduction

The romance of medieval Foolery is that Court Fools or Jesters were licensed to utter in public, under guise of entertainment yet with ludic, even sexual lucidity and devastating wit, home truths to Kings and other holders of power. Taking Liberties Theatre Company tried to put such a seriously Foolish sensibility into play in 1990's Australia. Having been invited by the editor of this volume to contribute a record of Taking Liberties, I will introduce the company with the following slogan or jingle, written as a description of the company for an Australian performing arts yearbook in the mid-1990s:

> Taking Liberties Theatre Company, Australia's Court Jester...poignantly mad, seriously funny, joyfully biting political theatre...see a Fool, break a rule, take a liberty...

In short, Taking Liberties aimed to be a political theatre company of a 'Foolish' kind - on posters and letterhead the heading 'Taking Liberties' is followed by the subtitle, 'a Foolish Theatre Company'.

In our era, I have long believed, theatre making is hobbled; crippled by the fact that *power has come to make extensive use of theatre and theatricality*. I am interested in Fooling as a motif, a tradition and a point of departure for theatre work because it offers a bridge between power and playing. Theatre making, for me, is *for* something. It is *for*, among other things, enquiring into power and the operations of power. It also is, or ought to be, a process for puncturing the thick clouds of illusion associated with the structures of our societies, the mode or instrument of puncture being playing.

My experiences as Artistic Director of Taking Liberties have clarified my thinking about both theatre and its predicament. This essay follows life by drawing upon episodes from the Taking Liberties story as points of entry to a larger discussion about theatre and its problematic position in contemporary society.

## Two Anecdotes

I begin with an effort to evoke the flavour and scope of the company with a couple of anecdotes. The first is from a time in the early 1990s when various people and I were having discussions about making our company's activities full-time. On one occasion, three of us were conversing together in my living room. One fellow, a former student of mine, spoke with great earnestness about taking the company on the road, touring the east coast of Australia, making good money. I interjected to say: 'We are very unlikely to make money. The theatre infrastructure is a stacked deck. The chances of us getting in and "making money" are only one in a hundred. At best, we'll be wiser eighteen months on'. Thus cautioned, my former student elected not to join us full-time!

The second anecdote, from several years later, is longer: an occasion when our manager, Ian McNish, met the then Senior Arts Policy Advisor to the new federal Australian Minister for Communications, Information Technology, and the Arts. McNish had been trying to meet the Senior Advisor, a young woman named Fiona Poletti, for some time. His objective was to put to her in person a scheme we had for systematically shattering the quangoesque structure of performing arts funding in Australia, and to replace it with another model aimed at launching many new theatre companies of many kinds and at making the finding of new audiences for theatre imperative. The seeming Quixote-like audacity of the manager of a small, unsubsidised theatre company making such a proposal to an arts bigwig did have one foot at least planted in reality. The two had spoken together on the phone quite a number of times, their conversations prompted by a steady stream of gadflyish op-ed articles on arts policy in *The Australian Financial Review* - the Aussie equivalent of the *Financial Times* - by myself. Mostly, these pieces had argued that the current system of Australian arts funding serves to prevent the performing arts from making social criticism with bite and to ensure that new audiences are not found, even as present ones dwindle. Many of the pieces directly addressed the federal arts minister by name, urging him to look at proposals of others and our own for change.

One Monday, then, the Senior Arts Advisor came to Brisbane from her base in Melbourne to have discussions with the local Arts establishment. She scheduled Taking Liberties' manager for a meeting at the coffee shop of the Brisbane Art Gallery, part of a much larger cultural campus wherein most of her meetings were taking place. Ian arrived at the gallery and waited at the arranged meeting spot. No Fiona. After a while, he phoned her on her mobile. Apparently, she was running late. He got the feeling she wanted to fob him off - this being quite a change from her previous tune. He pushed a little. She responded by suggesting that they meet for a few minutes in the reception area outside the director of the art gallery's office, whom she was to meet next.

A bit of further relevant background detail here is that, a few days before, on the Friday, the *Financial Review* had published a piece of mine strongly critical of the inaugural Brisbane Festival for its lack of grassroots participation, excessive cost and unusual financing (the local Performing Arts complex budget surplus was raided to the tune of several million dollars to pay for much of it, making it appear that the government subsidy was much less than it actually was). No doubt this piece offended a few of the local powers-that-be and in particular, the State Government's Arts Advisor, whom our manager had been lobbying about something else.

Back now to the Senior Arts Policy Advisor and the Taking Liberties manager standing together in front of the Gallery Director's PA's desk. The PA goes to tell the Director that Ms. Poletti has arrived and Ian launches into our proposal for a think tank-cum-hit squad on arts funding practices. He pushes her to state the government's likely response to his proposal. Fiona appears distracted, says that the Minister is not ready to go down the road advocated in the *Financial Review* articles at present. The PA returns, indicates that the Director is available and waiting. Fiona says she'll be a few more minutes. She then says to Ian, 'I'm told Taking Liberties doesn't really exist. They say you don't do any shows'. Ian replies, 'We are not part of the art scene. We survive by bringing theatre to people who don't go to theatre. On Saturday night, for instance, I was up until 3 a.m. bumping out a cabaret Taking Liberties put on that evening at a golf club (Nambour Golf Club 100 miles north of Brisbane)'. Fiona stares, not knowing what to make of this statement. The Director of the galley appears, interrupts with commanding presence, says that he's got another meeting to go to soon. Ms. Poletti follows him down the corridor.

These scenes, I hope, have begun to evoke Taking Liberties: marginality, alongside a measure of media presence. Invisibility - near zero networking - within the arts scene, together with a peculiar, interactive, disruptive effort, in person, through the media and, as I will come to momentarily, through our shows, at inducing change through and from government. And above all perhaps, a trademark habit of putting on productions in non-conventional and out of the way, yet mainstream places before audiences who normally avoid theatre as elitist - and too expensive.

*That's Twice*: A Foolish Play

The cast of *That's Twice* at its world premiere, Parliament House, Canberra:

Michael Earnshaw (Murray Torso)
Heather Johansen (Bronwyn B.)
Steve Hyde (Keith R.)
Tim Marchant
Margaret Marchant (singer)
Rebecca Byrne (singer)
Dennis Byrne (musician)
Georgina Morris
Set designed by Steve Burrows and Gunduz Kalic.
Directed by Gunduz Kalic

In this section, I tell of the life and times of *That's Twice,* a play that had its world premiere before an audience of politicians at Australia's Parliament House in Canberra in November 1993. *That's Twice* was written and cast by Taking Liberties company member Michael Earnshaw and myself with the Australian federal government of the time closely - but not solely - in mind. The play's jokes were updated nightly, according to political developments on the day.

The piracy/smuggling of *That's Twice* into Parliament House stands out as one of Taking Liberties most purely Foolish deeds, inasmuch as the play was designed for a Parliamentary audience - and preferably, one including the Prime Minister and Cabinet. The play having been written and rehearsals having been started, the trick was to 'book' Parliament House - and entice in the targeted audience. Then company manager Louise Earnshaw gained sponsorship for Parliamentary performance of the play - a first - through Queensland Senator Margaret Reynolds. The basis upon which the play was sold and accepted was as a kind of cultural delegation, a celebration of regional Australia. We had succeeded in booking our venue - and at a time Parliament was sitting. Rehearsals concluded and costumes and sets manufactured, many donations from local businesses in Bundaberg, Queensland, the Company's then base, having been solicited and received. Before the company departed, the play was road tested in a dress rehearsal before a local audience, members of which were asked to fill out a questionnaire afterwards. The survey clearly showed that the audience understood this was a play highly critical of the government. Once in Canberra, the company set up shop in Senator Reynolds office, using it as a base to entice politicians to see the show and to garner media publicity. Posters were put up throughout the Parliamentary precinct.

Finally, the day of performance arrived. First, a matinee dress rehearsal was put on, consisting of an abridged 45 minute version of the play. This took place in a Parliamentary courtyard, before an audience of media workers and parliamentary workers eating their lunches outside. The performance was received warmly and with much laughter. So far, so good. The risk, of course, was that at any stage, officials would 'catch on' to our message and halt our evening performance for the MPs. In the event, the evening performance, in an awkward space with bad acoustics, went ahead. Many politicians from both government and opposition benches came, though not the Prime Minister or any Government Ministers. Within ten minutes, many of these politicians had walked out. A few opposition members remained, laughing uproariously, presumably recognising antics of the government in the action. The performance of *That's Twice: A Foolish Play* was taped in its entirety by ABC-TV, Australia's main public broadcaster. The cameraman who filmed the play quite seriously asked cast members after the show, 'What are you trying to do, start a war?' In the next day's *Canberra Times* its theatre reviewer wrote favourably of the play, saying among other things that the nations' 'political powerbrokers had been lambasted in their own den'. Subsequently, *The Australian* was to write that 'the play is a two-fingered riposte from Australia's forgotten people delivered with enough cartoonish energy to fuel our manufacturing industries for a year, if we had any'. That reviewer also singled out a 'talent-plus' Margaret Marchant and the 'best fat suit ever'.

What did politicians and others who were in the audience for *That's Twice* see? The play was satirical, obviously, the style of performance drawing from contemporary stand-up comedy, *commedia del'arte*, rap music *circa* 1993 and epic structure. The play begins with an enormous build up to the arrival onstage of the lead character, President Murray Torso, evidently a politician/cult figure. Torso announces that the government of which he is the head will lock itself - and all elected politicians - up in jail to put a stop to political corruption for once and for all. The money saved on royal commissions is to be used 'to upgrade conditions in prison'. From their base in prison, Torso and his colleagues proceed to sell the country they govern and its people on the open world market to the highest bidder. The unemployed, for instance - there was considerable unemployment at the time - are to be drowned and turned into a tourist attraction, namely an artificial reef. One of the plays' chief targets was multiculturalism, as used and abused by the Labour government of the time. From a Foolish perspective, the play was arguably a prescient 'whisper of warning' to government, years ahead of time, of the coming rise of Hansonism and of the backlash of country Australia against the overzealous application of policies associated with globalisation. Had the 'political powerbrokers' listened to and heeded our Foolish whisper, policy u-turns could have taken place earlier - and much grief been spared.

Upon return to Bundaberg, I was satisfied with the event, with both the performance and the publicity received, though the latter was confined only, as noted above, to the arts pages. Despite our efforts at bringing the *That's Twice* event to the attention of the Parliamentary press gallery, members of which professed interest and sympathy and admiration for what we were doing, and thus gaining wider media exposure, the company met with little success in this respect. The company did manage, however, to be hired as entertainers at the birthday party of the child of one of the nations' leading political commentators - and thus gaining a few dollars toward the trips expenses, otherwise met by the cast, crew and well-wishers.

The subsequent career of *That's Twice* involved two major rewritings followed by subsequent workshopping and the inclusion of additional cast member Donna Hickey in order to keep the play in tune with Australian political developments. Performances were put on in Bundaberg and in Brisbane; *That's Twice 2* playing a season in 1995 at Van Gogh's Earlobe and *That's Twice 3* playing in 1996 at the Sit-down Comedy Club. Additionally, as featured in an SBS *Imagine* programme documentary segment on Taking Liberties and on the front pages of the Bundaberg *News-Chronicle*, characters from the show crashed public events with exquisite timing, upstaging leading political figures such as the Premier of Queensland and the Prime Minister of Australia. Thereby, the world was turned momentarily topsy-turvy in a manner evocative of the medieval Feast of Fools. 1997 saw characters from the show performing in a regular short segment on ABC-TV's *Stateline*, Queensland's weekly state current affairs round-up programme by lampooning politics of the moment. In that year, we also proposed to a leading, influential supporter of the Federal government that the company be hired to be a resident company of Fools at the federal Parliament. The offer was declined, satire being described in the refusal as an offensive and culturally dangerous genre. The words of John Ralston Saul are perhaps an appropriate close to this section on *That's Twice*, 'Even the fool is banished from the castles of modern power'.

## Theatre/Power

Power is a word strongly associated with Michel Foucault. Foucault considered that there was no intellectual stance that offered a perfectly impartial position with which to view or judge the workings of power. No position is uncompromised, all knowledge and discourse being caught up in the 'web of power'. Equally, for Foucault there is no sovereign subject. Rather, human subjectivity, at least since the sixteenth century in the West, is fashioned by the actions of 'governmentality' - a concept I will discuss further below - in managing populations and training citizens. Nonetheless, he considered that freedom lies in thought - inasmuch as thought affords the individual the opportunity of changing his or her behaviour from what it otherwise might unthinkingly be - and in 'parhesis', the free speech of the citizen speaking out to his or her government. In his own scholarship, Foucault sought to support thought and parhesis through his genealogies, which tracked how particular practices of power had come to be.

I like to ask: do our theatre policies and practices facilitate or hinder thinking and speaking out on the part of theatre companies? In this section, I consider this question both as a general issue and in relation to Taking Liberties.

John Ralston Saul, in his homage to the novel as the most difficult-to-control instrument of public communication, states that in comparison the theatre is readily controllable. Its dependence upon buildings, equipment, place and time of performance, he considers, means that the authorities can easily contain it. Indeed, from one perspective the history of the theatre can be read as the history of its containment by the authorities. Civil and religious authorities have often found theatre to be an unpalatable pastime - and one threatening to public order. Theatre regulation throughout history has largely been preoccupied with containing the vitality and influence of live drama. Jonas Barish argues that:

> the stage provokes the most active and sustained hostility when it becomes a vital force. It is then that its own values seem most dangerously to collide with the received values of church and state. The denunciations of the Fathers... would make no sense except as a response to the vigorous theatrical institutions of the day. (*The anti theatrical prejudice*, 1981: 66)

Such denunciations have often led to theatre closures, for example and famously, the Puritan shutdown of the Elizabethan/Jacobean popular theatre, a shutdown that lasted eighteen years. In short, the history of the stage can be seen as interplay between theatre as an unruly and licentious popular cultural form and theatre policies as a means of control and/or facilitation of the form.

The current state of affairs, however, is somewhat different. I argue that theatre is now more a part of than it is contained by power. To support this argument, I will draw upon Foucault's framework of governmentality. He coined the term to encapsulate his understanding of the way in which power has come to operate. Briefly, Foucault's view was that societies function not simply through impositions of the state as a central organ or entity, but rather through a 'web of power' reaching far beyond Government *per se* (1984: 58). In his essay, 'On Governmentality' Foucault identified a historical shift occurring from the middle of the sixteenth century, in which the human populations of European societies emerge as objects of active management. Indeed, he argues, the engendering of economy and order in and through the population becomes the chief business of increasingly centralised state administrations. Paradoxically, however, the state is by no means all-powerful. Foucault writes:

> I don't want to say that the state isn't important, what I want to say is that relations of power, and hence the analysis that must be made of them, necessarily extend beyond the limits of the state. In two senses: first of all because the state, for all the omnipotence of its apparatuses, is far from being able to occupy the whole field of actual power relations, and further, because the state can only operate on the basis of other, already existing power relations. (1984: 64)

Since Foucault's death, others, such as the sociologist Nikolas Rose, have elaborated on his work. Rose argues that governmentality or 'governmentalisation of the state' is associated with the harnessing of 'microfields of power...to enable the extension of control over space and time - or what I have termed government at a distance' (1999: 22). Rose has conducted much research into psychology, drawing out its origins as a discipline and explicating its evolving contribution to government at a distance through the fashioning of human subjectivity since World War Two.

My own interest lies in the performing arts as mode and aspect of governance at a distance. Since World War Two, the links between government and the arts have grown steadily, to the point where now there is a thick intermeshing of structures and practices. Governments grant subsidies on the basis of policy rationales, which in turn are associated with board appointments and guidelines for grant approvals and renewals, all of which tend strongly to shape and influence the content and style of the work that is produced by arts companies. Through networked government at a distance, including peer assessment, governments are having a hand in directing the shows that audiences watch! In short, *independent* 'speaking out' is not on the agenda but rather is muted, silenced even before the impulse towards it can form by the prevalence and influence of what are effectively arts quangoes.

Worse still, the association with government gives an imprint of legitimacy and respectability to subsidised companies which has the effect of making the position of companies who do attempt to speak out, such as Taking Liberties, more marginal and difficult than it would otherwise be. The silence and respectability - or trendy-commentary-within-appropriate-bounds - of the government-sponsored companies amount to a dead weight upon the body politic that cancels out debate by setting too preformed and narrow an agenda for it. If the government subsidised companies were not in existence, the marketplace of ideas within the arts would be more lively and critical. At the least, we ought to be applying the thought of Foucault by searching for ways to multiply and make discontinuous centres of power so as not to facilitate or manage but to allow the possibility of more speaking out by arts companies. And to allow these voices to more readily draw audiences; to allow these voices to be more readily heard.

## Open Performance Cabaret

How did Taking Liberties survive financially? The company was/is an unsubsidised one, surviving only by virtue of the 'hard yakka', to use the Australian vernacular phrase for very hard work, of its members - including their salesmanship in booking shows. There was no money to be made from political Foolery, such as *That's Twice* - that was clear from the first dress rehearsal showing of the play in Bundaberg. Our usual audience was happy enough to be invited to see the work, but to pay for it was something else. Elsewhere, takings from audiences were good compared to those enjoyed by small, unsubsidised companies in the Queensland marketplace, but not sufficient to pay bills and wages. To support itself, the company undertook what I call open performance cabaret. This work is similar to Fooling in method, but with little or no contemporary political content.

The best point of entry to the open performance cabaret of Taking Liberties is perhaps our adaptation of *Taming of the Shrew*, first rehearsed in early 1994. Associate Director of Taking Liberties, Heather Johansen (Kate), Michael Earnshaw (Petruchio) and Steven Hyde (Host of the Evening, Christopher Sly, Hortensio, Grumio and more) worked under my direction to shorten the play and turn it into a musical three hander. Assisted by singer-songwriter and guitarist Andrea Farmer and soon to be musical director Dennis Byrne, the cast and I created songs to punctuate and heighten the dramatic action, drawing lyrics from lines from Shakespeare. The production was set in a boxing ring, a fact that was to be reported in the Sydney *Sun-Herald*, and first performed in a large room underneath the grandstand of the Bundaberg Showgrounds. Our *Shrew* was played with a twist, Petruchio's effort at dominating succeeding completely, till the very end of the play, when she turns the tables utterly.

I will now describe the development of the open performance cabaret style by relating the impressions of an associate uninvolved in the making of the *Shrew* who saw it on opening night and again, several months later, at the Bundaberg Rugby Club. The atmosphere in our barn-cum-playhouse immediately after the opening night show, according to the perceptions of this colleague, was quite full of feeling. For all the pleasure in the evening, all the laughter throughout, there was a poignant awkwardness in the room, as the women and men in the audience felt the cast return to everyday reality, felt their presence together as men and women, and felt the show's connection to the sexual politics of their own lives. The show had made people feel in a public setting, not something they were used to - and this was a little uncomfortable. In contrast, the performance at the Rugby Club several months later, after a season at the Showground venue and several touring performances, including one to teenagers at a high school and another before an audience of senior citizens, was reportedly carnivalesque. My associate found the rugby club *Shrew* to be a revelation. In one moment early on he experienced the show as explosively folding out from the stage into the room, expanding in size so as to contain within it the entirety of the room and its audience - notwithstanding the noise from the club bar next door. The reaction of the audience was ecstatic, participatory. The show was a performed narrative, watched passively, if feelingly, by the audience no longer. The imaginary world within the show - Shakespeare's fair Verona - was a place the audience was transported to no longer. Rather, this night's *Shrew* was stand up comedy; was an event that took place not behind a conventionalised fourth wall but profoundly, absorbedly *in the room here and now*. This *Shrew* excited bodies in the audience to jump up and momentarily insert themselves in the action uninvited and unrehearsed, yet with perfect grace. This *Shrew* freed tongues in the audience to go far beyond any conventionalised audience participation and made them loquacious and boldly witty to match Shakespeare. This *Shrew* played not to but vigorously *with* its audience - and its audience played equally vigorously in response - including with one another. When the show was done and dusted, its content and import were dissolved: all was happy, content, full. 'First time I ever understood Shakespeare', said one man to me in passing, on his way out.

The 'three dimensional' rugby club *Shrew*, which was taped by SBS-TV, Australia's multicultural broadcaster, was indeed a breakthrough, the culmination of much, much work on the part of the cast and myself in developing the open performance cabaret style. This style is anti-theatrical. It involves the player in a moment-by-moment shying away from 'acting' (that is, away from the splits of consciousness whereby part of the self convinces itself, and tries to convince the audience, that it and the character and are one and the same) and towards an opening out of the performance. By 'opening out', I mean a continuous infusion into the rehearsed action of the paradoxical, precarious passion of playing. I, you, we; players are connected to one another and to the audience by live, unpredictable flows of recognition that we are simultaneously then and there in the illusion *and* here and now in this place together. In other words, the unfolding performance is not a convincing alternate reality in which we are immersed, but rather a game we are taking part in with serious, joyful intent. Methodologically, the influences here are again stand-up comedy, commedia, epic structure and the broad movement away from the proscenium arch and its pacification of the audience.

Our *Shrew*, incidentally, played to full houses. In Bundaberg, a sugar and rum centre cum retirement colony on the mid Queensland coast, we had from 1991 built up a devoted following for our cabarets, which were performed intermittently. One gentleman in particular, the British expatriate owner of a local steel home construction franchise, was not exceptional in saying, 'I came to the first show with a party of four, the following show with eight, the show after that with eighteen and next time I'm going to book the whole night out!' Nonetheless, as the company went full-time, it sought a larger horizon. In late 1994, the company moved its base from the Bundaberg Showground to a premise with a room big enough to turn into a theatre space above a vehicle upholsterer in Fortitude Valley in Brisbane, capital of Queensland and with a metropolitan area of about 1.5 million people, in late 1994.

From Brisbane, the company near-continuously toured its cabaret shows to hotels and licensed clubs. The Bribie Island Returned Services League, Nambour Golf Club, Cleveland Hotel, Keperra Waters Hotel and Deception Bay Sporting Club are the names of a few of the venues. The steadily growing repertoire of shows included the *Taming of the Shrew* and *The Country Wife*, as well the company's own creations: *Carnivale*, *Stick 'em Up*, *Arrividerci Mama*, *Internationale*, *L'escargot a go go*, *Fiesta* and *On the Wallaby*, a reinvention of the Australian music hall. One of the most popular productions was *Folti Towirs Bombay*, a work initially commissioned by a hotel chain. Inspired by the television series of similar name, our *Folti Towirs Bombay* was set in an Australian expatriate's restaurant in India. Demand for the cabarets was such that on many occasions, the company split into two or three troupes in order to serve several venues simultaneously. Many bookings were return bookings; many bookings were by the recommendation of one venue to another. New shows were added to the repertoire to meet demand. Most often Taking Liberties toured, but it also booked audiences into its own venue in the Valley and to a larger venue in a club nearby.

In content, many of the cabarets were comedic explorations of cultural identity in a country with migrants from many lands and the highest rate of intermarriage between ethnicities in the world. Those audience members who were migrants from the region of the world being celebrated in a given show often enjoyed the shows most of all. In tone, the shows were warm-hearted and big-hearted. Although the stand up comedy element within the shows grew, audiences were never ridiculed. Our players always made fools of themselves first and most. The upshot of the open performance cabarets was that on many occasions, with many audiences, Taking Liberties took important steps towards achieving in a small way a renewal of popular theatre: that is, theatre as an uproarious, earthily ribald and irresistible place of delight for ordinary people. The practice of doing so many of these shows, full as they were of witty spontaneous interchange between players and players and audience, enriched performances of *That's Twice* and later Foolish works by giving the players much experience in keeping a light, quick touch. The money earned from the cabarets enabled the company to pay its members minimal wages - thus we survived.

## Theatre in it and up against it

Four and five decades ago, Jerzy Grotowski began his quest to identify what in theatre was not duplicable by film and television. I share this quest, if not the direction Grotowski took in his own search. I think that we need, however, a working definition of what theatre *was*. I follow Victor Turner in thinking that theatre is strongly associated with *social 'metacommentary'* (Turner 1982: 104). Turner writes that the plays of Sophocles and Aristophanes were intensely reflexive. If they were 'mirrors held up to nature (or rather to society and culture) they were active...mirrors, mirrors that probed and analysed the axioms and assumptions of the social structure, isolated the building blocks of the culture' (1982: 104).

In other words, theatre, at best, has offered a place and a means by which societies may reflect upon themselves. As an institution containing the potential for reflection or social metacommentary, theatre is at its optimum as a popular art, as a meeting place for representative cross sections of society, where the public can participate in the making and remaking of a common culture. For instance, as Saul has argued in regards to sixteenth and seventeenth century theatre:

> No one would have been able to distinguish between theatre for the elites and theatre for the people. The various parts of the audience took what suited them from plays like *King Lear* and *Hamlet*, whose staying power still seems to come in large part from this populist conception. (1991: 546)

Clearly, theatre is a popular art no longer - and has not been for some time. But how did this state of things - the predicament I referred to earlier - come to pass? I argue that we can, in part, begin to trace out theatre's predicament by reflecting, with Raymond Williams, that drama can be equated with theatre no longer. Generations of human beings have, since the advent of film and broadcasting, grown up imbibing most of their diet of drama from other sources. Theatre was hit hard by this change, and especially by the advent of television, which increased the amount of drama consumed on a daily basis by ordinary people to a level far beyond that supplied by theatre in any society or historical period.

So drama had taken on a new importance in everyday life. What function, what new need, was the increase in drama fulfilling?

In their own ways, a number of thinkers have attempted to address this question. Perhaps this most succinct is that of Manuel Castells. He writes that we have achieved a state of *real virtuality*:

> [ours] is a system in which reality itself (that is, people's material symbolic existence) is entirely captured, fully immersed in a virtual image setting, in the world of make-believe, in which appearances are not just on the screen through which make-believe is communicated, but they become the experience. (1996: 373)

Castells argues that manufactured appearances have become the stuff of experience. I add that appearances are in large measure *constructed through the application of drama and performance to film, broadcasting, the built environment and new media*. In short, instead of being utilised voluntarily, as a probing if sometimes uncomfortable mirror, and hence being aligned to the possibility of change, theatricality is being used simultaneously as a primary social glue and an imposing tool of persuasion and control and thus has itself become a new status quo.

I am passing very quickly over this immense and subtle subject, which I call the theatricalisation of life, to come to the nub: theatre's predicament is in the position of competing with its own shadow, theatricality at large, a shadow which dwarfs it utterly and which has a different purpose. In fact, theatre mostly does not attempt to compete, or to stand back for distance, but instead serves. In the post-war era, as the Encyclopedia Brittanica of 1960 notes, many expected that theatre would 'finally die' as an art form in the face of the powerful new competitor-suppliers of drama. But theatre did not die. Rather, except in a few commercial centres such as London's West End and New York's Broadway, it was preserved as a kind of living museum through various schemes of governmental and corporate subsidy - the clear reality being that most companies could not survive on their own box office. The result, notwithstanding the outstanding efforts of myriad small companies in trying to go against the tide, is, as has been well documented, a theatre infrastructure weighed down by recycled nineteenth century values of aesthetic excellence and drawing its audience from a dwindling minority of the population. With its bias towards the aesthetic rather than the social, such theatre effectively goes along with the theatricalisation of life without thinking about it. The theatre infrastructure also tends to serve the usage of theatricality by power by acting as a training and proving ground for talent.

## Beginnings and Endings?

In 1996, alongside its other activities, the company had devised and put on a studio production of its work *Gulls*, featuring singer-songwriter Andrea Farmer. This play depicted the crushing of a group of misfits, who lived together in a loose community in a large salvage yard outside of planning laws. Shortly afterwards, we heard that a similar, real life community was being evicted from land on one of the islands near Brisbane. 1997 and 1998 saw Taking Liberties devote much time to intensively workshop three play concepts of mine. One of these was *Hones T,* a grotesquely black depiction of the use of show business and performance techniques by elites. As part of the process, artist Steve Burrows completed an extensive series of paintings as backdrops to the studio performance, many of which featured a Blair-like character. Another, *Virtual Tramps*, explores the use of the persona of the 'old tramp' as a device for breaking down the wall between performers and audience. The third, *Don Cullote* is an updating of the Don Quixote myth to contemporary times, and set in contemporary political context.

The origins of Taking Liberties lay in graduate companies formed in Australia's Northern Territory in the mid to late 1980s by former students of mine. These companies played in outback pubs, on cattle stations and homesteads and in Aboriginal communities and outstations. One company in particular, TAE, also played to tens of thousands of schools students in the Northern Territory and Queensland. It was the core members of such companies that evolved into Taking Liberties in Bundaberg in the early 1990s. By the end of 1999, after years of hard yakka and a few too many bump-ins and outs, some full time company members were growing tired - including of being permanently 'broke'. A few had left to try their hand in advertising and other fields. It was time for us to gear down, time for us to reflect on what had been achieved so far and what we as a company and as individuals hoped to do next.

## The Passion of the Real

Saul has written that the greatest play of the twentieth century is Beckett's *Waiting for Godot*, because it depicts, in his view, the individual's discovery that he is somehow unreal. In writing of the theatricalisation of life phenomenon, the Slovenian philosopher Zizek says that:

> precisely because the universe in which we live is somehow a universe of dead conventions and artificiality, the only authentic real experience must be some extremely violent, shattering experience. And this we experience as a sense that now we are back in real life.

This violent countertendency to the unreality of the theatricalisation of life is the passion of the real. Zizek gives as one instance the fact that there are thousands of 'cutters' in America. These people, mainly women but also men, ritually cut themselves with razors, not out of pure masochism, but to feel themselves to be real.

For me, theatre generally *isn't*, but readily *can be* a non-violent passion for the real, a way towards discovering that we are bodies here together with public concerns. I believe that this was the passion that drove Taking Liberties in Australia in the 1990s; was the passion that awoke and thrilled in its audiences.

# Parachuting In: Issues Arising from Drama as Intervention within Communities in Azerbaijan

Velda Harris

> We must ask ourselves not only what we are doing, but also how we are doing it. Are such projects actually fostering understanding and cultural sharing or are they merely reifying hegemonic structures and painful misconceptions. (Conceison 1995: 151)

The article will explore issues arising from the adaptation of British models of drama and Theatre in Education, first in work devised for refugee children in a London school; and secondly, during short visits over a three year period, in work with young people in displaced persons' camps in Azerbaijan. It starts with a discussion of the principles underlying TIE (Theatre in Education) practice, then turns to the growing body of literature on intercultural theatre practice to provide a framework for the consideration of issues important during the development of the project. These include: consultation and collaboration as a means of identifying an appropriate 'learning area' or theme for the work; the relationship between the source culture and the target audience; models of intercultural theatre practice; communication without language; and audience response. The discussion will then be related to four case studies - collaborative work in an intercultural setting produced by students in their second year on the BA Drama and Education course at the Central School of Speech and Drama.

## Theatre in Education Practice

It is not my intention here to give an account of the development of TIE (Bolton, Hornbrook, Elwell, Jackson) but to isolate the underlying principles that informed the work, particularly in the early idealistic period of the 1970s and 1980s when companies including the Belgrade, Coventry, Greenwich Young People's Theatre, Leeds TIE and the Sheffield Crucible TIE were formulating policy and practice, supported by the parent house and generous LEA funding. Tony Jackson defines the TIE programme:

> ...not as a 'one off' event that is here today and gone tomorrow, but a carefully structured pattern of activities, usually devised and researched by the company, around a topic of relevance both to the school curriculum and to the children's own lives, pre-

sented in school by the company and involving the children directly in an experience of the situations and problems that the topic throws up. (Jackson 1993: 4)

In best practice, early consultation meeting between the TIE company and the teachers and Head Teachers from local schools would identify an appropriate theme or learning area which would provide a starting point for research and the beginning of the devising process. Teachers would be kept informed about the development of the work and involved in the 'structured pattern of activities' before the team's arrival in the school and after the visit, with the help of resource packs provided by the company. While the resource packs were likely to include factual information and a variety of information relating to the topic, the use of dramatic form meant that the topic was explored through the experience of characters involved in the action, with whom the young audience were likely to identify and empathise. It also meant that those devising the play would have made a decision about the frame or viewpoint from which the topic would be explored.

This is a familiar and generally accepted feature of theatre for adults, as in canonical plays like *The Doll's House, The Good Person of Setzuan, Death of a Salesman* and more recent plays like Mark Ravenhill's *Shopping and Fucking* in which social and political mores are held up for scrutiny through the experience of central characters. But, when a similar process was adopted in plays for young people, and presented as Theatre in Education in statutory or related educational settings, accusations of bias, political motivation and indoctrination were quick to creep in. David Pammenter, writing in 1980, addresses this issue:

> The devising team must have a clear perspective of the purpose and function of their work before they start devising at all - in the same way as a conscientious teacher or writer has. They must have a clear idea of the forces at work both on themselves and on the children they wish to work with, and a real awareness of the parameters or confines set on their work by the morals, values and ethics of the society we live in whether or not these are to be subsequently challenged. (Cited in Jackson 1993: 63)

This statement anticipates the concerns expressed by Conceison at the head of the article. It reminds us of the importance of research, consultation, reflection and ongoing debate as an essential part of involvement in TIE; and that what is a complex endeavour in the familiar arena of the British educational system is further complicated and politicised when translated to an intercultural context.

## Between the Ideal and the Realisation Falls the Shadow: twenty years on

In Pammenter's analysis the devising team adopts the role of 'the conscientious teacher or writer' who decides the perspective that will be taken on the topic explored. There is no commitment to the presentation of balanced arguments, and the perspective taken is likely to challenge rather than reinforce establishment attitudes. The process is intended to 'enable the child to discover his or her responses - it is to do with liberating one's responses rather than rather than imposing order' (Jackson 1993: 63). It is interesting to see this process realised in representative TIE plays of the 1970s and to observe the shift to multiple perspectives (or the presentation of balanced arguments) in some plays of the late 1990s. In the first part of *Rare Earth* (Belgrade, Coventry, 1974), set on the American plains, the Indian Earth Spirit, Wakatanka, describes the violation of her land; and in a robust, farcical second half, the anachronistic, English tourist family, the Ramsbottoms, set in motion a sequence of destruction that includes deforestation, the destruction of agricultural land, invasive mining and pollution of the environment. Since the family is only concerned with getting rich quick, the play is a serious indictment of global capitalism and the destruction of the environment. While the play is both sensitive to the issues and highly entertaining, the voice of the capitalist 'other' is expressed only through parody. In Leeds TIE's *Raj,* colonialism and the beginnings of the Indian independence movement are viewed from the perspective of a young Indian girl (the narrator, performed by an Indian member of the company) growing up under the colonial regime. The traditional Eurocentric 'take' on events of the period is replaced by a perspective which represents the 'other' as individuals subject to the colonial experience and also, by association, the 'other' in the intracultural sense of second generation ethnic Indians growing up in Leeds. The inversion of the traditional, authorised viewpoint is a deliberate choice by the devisers intended to redress a perceived imbalance: the British colonisers are presented as paternalistic, aloof, snobbish and insensitive.

In leaping forward twenty years to the end of the century, the climate of political and economic constraint in education as well as the Arts, has had its effect on the funding and artistic policy of theatre companies who have inherited the mantle of TIE. Survival has depended on carving out a niche that can be justified in a market economy where competitive applications for grants and accountability to funding bodies have replaced a freer *modus operandi.* If we turn to current TIE practice we can find examples of work in which multiple perspectives on an issue are presented. Y-Touring, a London based company, supported by the Wellcome Trust and the Office of Science and Technology, 'supports the key educational aims of both organisations, including making science more accessible to young people, increasing scientific literacy and addressing the ethical and social issues raised by biomedical research' (Flyer, Creating the Debate for the New Millennium, Y-Touring 2001). Y-Touring commissions plays which disseminate information about scientific and medical issues, and use theatrical form as way of personalising and problematising ethical debate. Rather than engaging in closure and the resolution of the problem, the play leaves the audience to make up their minds on the basis of the evidence, both factual and personal, explored in the play. 'We aim to create high quality theatre and drama which highlights important, often difficult issues and empowers our audiences to generate change in themselves, others and society' (Y-Touring 2001) In *Pig in the Middle*, which explores issues surrounding xenotransplantation, each of the characters provides a different perspective on the problem: the vegetarian, animal-loving girl who will not improve her condition at the expense of an animal's suffering; the boy who wants to escape invasive hospital procedures and live a normal life; the mother who agonises by proxy; and the doctor who is concerned for medical ethics. While this kind of structure is very effective in communicating information and providing a stimulus for debate, the affective model of TIE described earlier is more likely to reach out across the cultural and linguistic divide to the target audiences for this project.

## Links to Interculturalism: the source and target culture

The issue of perspective is of fundamental importance in the consideration of theatre in an intercultural context. Discussion of Leeds TIE's *Raj* has already suggested that the frame or viewpoint from which historical material is approached can challenge hegemonic assumptions in a multi-cultural setting. It has become common currency in discussion of intercultural theatre practice to distinguish between a source culture from which a particular theatrical performance is derived and a target culture in which the 'translated' performance is presented to an audience. In his concept of the 'hourglass of cultures' Pavis (1992: 4) identifies twelve filters passed through as a theatrical performance moves from one culture to the other. While this relates mainly to work that is transformed (like Peter Brook's *Mahabarata*) into a hybrid form in the course of its passage, the idea of the filters is applicable to the drama project, although in this case the source culture is British and the target culture is Azeri. It is a cultural and artistic model from a British source that will undergo the process of adaptation. This will be determined by the 'perspective of the adapters' (the students involved in the project) whose choice of form and content will be informed by their research into the artistic, social and cultural models provided by the target culture. In deciding on an appropriate holding form they will need to consider what 'reception adapters' they can build into the work and the readability of the performance. The complexities involved in 'translating' a performance from a source to a target culture are further complicated in this case by the fact that the 'perspective of the adapters' includes an educational methodology, and by the particular experience and needs of the target audience.

Azerbaijan has for centuries been subject to invasion, conquest and domination by cultural 'others'. Its boundaries have constantly shifted, as has the ethnic composition of its inhabitants. It became a Soviet Republic in 1920, subject to communist rule from Moscow. In addition to the imposition of a 'foreign' political and economic system, Soviet influence is seen in the secularisation of the society, the emergence of a dominant Russian speaking ruling class, the import of Russian cultural models and a prescribed education curriculum. In 1988 a local war broke out between Azeri and Armenian nationals living in the fertile border region of Nagorno Karabakh. This escalated when American-trained Armenian troops invaded the area, and many Azeris were killed or driven from their homes to take refuge in the capital, Baku, and elsewhere. This fuelled the Independence movement and led to strikes and demonstrations in the streets. In January 1990, Soviet tanks entered Baku to suppress the uprising, and after four days of anarchy, the Kremlin issued a press release 'regretting' the deaths of 69 civilians and 14 military in what it described as a 'security operation to constrain hooliganism and Islamic extremism in Azerbaijan'(van der Leeuw 2000). Several thousand ethnic

Azeri people, many of whom lost loved ones during the war, fled from their homeland in Nagorno Karabakh and became refugees in their own country. Since the economy of the country, particularly in Baku, could not sustain this large influx of homeless and dependent people, they have been living, since 1993, in displaced persons' camps run by foreign agencies like the International Federation of the Red Cross.

In any kind of intercultural encounter the participants carry with them the accumulated baggage of history and its scarcely recognised manifestations in contemporary attitudes and behaviour. In talking about 'the relationship of the "West" and its dominated cultural Others', Edward Said refers to 'an unequal relationship between unequal interlocutors' (Said 1993: 191). Our relationship with the target audience for the drama project was not in this instance predicated on a history of colonial encounters. We were working under the aegis of the Leonard Cheshire Centre for Conflict Recovery, which was set up in 1997 'to study the medical consequences of war and disaster and to establish standards of best practice' (Kennedy 1999: 9). The project developed a Fast Track Referral System, which has 'provided over 200 life- or limb-saving operations to date' (Kennedy, 1999: 9) and also funded the drama project. The medical and logistics team had already established an excellent relationship with the people in the camps, which acknowledged and respected the 'other' culture as well as providing much-needed medical aid. In this ethos we hoped to be able to work in a way that minimised any perceived inequality.

## Examples of Intercultural Theatre Practice: taking to/from/universals

It may be helpful at this point to consider some examples of intercultural theatre practice, in its considerable diversity, and to ask what the intentions of the practitioners were, how they worked, and what the response of the audience was. A considerable amount of discussion has surrounded the issue of appropriation: practitioners who have taken *from* a source culture and adapted either a text, or a style of performance, or the visual aspects of performance. Bharucha (1996) suggests a reason for this:

> ...one could argue that interculturalism was born out of a sort of *ennui*, a reaction to aridity and the subsequent search for a new source of energy, vitality and sensuality through the incorporation of 'rejuvenating' raw materials. (Bharucha, in Pavis 1996: 207)

Ironically, this process of 'taking from' another culture often starts from respect and admiration and the desire to incorporate elements of the source culture into new or hybridized work. This is seen in the plays of Brecht and Yeats, in the productions of Brook, Mnouchkine and Robert Wilson. Richard Schechner finds this something to rejoice about:

There was something celebratory about discovering how diverse the world was, how many performance genres there were and how we could enrich our own experience by borrowing, stealing, exchanging. (Schechner 1982: 19)

It is only when we hear the voice of the 'other' raised in objection that we begin to consider the legitimacy of this process. This voice has been strongly raised in response to Peter Brook's theatrical reworking of the great Indian epic poem, the *Mahabharata*. Bharucha (1990) sees the adaptation as 'a cultural salad of which [Brook] is the unacknowledged chef'.

The *Mahabharata* is not merely a great narrative poem; it is our itihasa, the fundamental source of knowledge of our literature, dance, painting, sculpture, theology, statecraft, sociology, economy - in short our history in all its detail and density. (Bharucha 1990: 69)

Probir Guha, director of the Living Theatre of West Bengal, where Brook did research for the *Mahabharata* in 1983, complains of feeling used and let down, 'We don't want to be exploited culturally, we don't want to be guinea pigs for experiments' (cited in Schechner 1977: 135). Gautam Dasgupta (1991) supports Bharucha's viewpoint, 'Brook's *Mahabharata* falls short of the essential Indianness of the epic by staging predominantly its major incidents and failing to adequately emphasize its coterminous philosophical precepts', but goes on to concede that, 'it does however raise the spectre, in no uncertain terms, of the fate that awaits us in the event of a nuclear holocaust' (Marranca & Dasgupta 1991: 81). If I invert the Pavis hourglass at this point in the discussion and consider my response to adaptations and re-workings of the Bible and Shakespeare (the twin poles of our cultural heritage and the closest we can get to the *Mahabharata* in Western culture) I cannot raise the same passionate concern as the Indian writers cited above and generally, even in a populist reworking of Shakespeare, like Baz Luhrmann's cinematic version of *Romeo and Juliet,* find there are interesting insights to be gained. My culturally conditioned belief in the indestructibility of these iconic texts is born of a history undisturbed, at least for the past millennium, by invasion, conquest or colonisation. Clearly, for the Indian writers cited above, as for the displaced people in Azerbaijan, the experience is different. While the Bible and Shakespeare have been translated into many languages, before Peter Brook the *Mahabharata* was known, in the West, only to scholars. Although in his foreword to the play version of the *Mahabharata*, Brook says, 'We have tried to suggest the flavour of India without pretending to be what we are not', Bharucha's sense of outrage is understandable. From his perspective, the *Mahabharata* was served up for consumption in the West by someone who did not understand its significance in its culture of origin and consequently misrepresented it. Pavis (1996), on the other hand, suggests that transformation is an inevitable part of intercultural performance, if a text from one culture is to be meaningful in another.

In the strictest sense, this creates hybrid forms drawing upon a more or less conscious and voluntary mixing of performance traditions traceable to distinct cultural areas. (Pavis 1996: 8).

It is this kind of hybrid that has emerged in preparing work for presentation in the Azeri camps.

As well as being concerned with taking *from* a source culture, intercultural theatre has engaged in taking theatre *to* target audiences in other cultures. Susan Bennett (1997) provides a definition of intercultural performance based on spectatorship: 'As it takes one spectator to make a performance, so it takes one culturally specific spectator to make an intercultural performance' (Bennett 1997: 171). This broadens the debate to include instances, for example in inner city schools, when a piece of theatre is performed to a multicultural audience, including refugees or recent immigrants. Said's notion of 'unequal interlocutors' rears its head again here, both in relation to the performance (say, by a visiting TIE company) which emanates from the dominant culture, and because of the relative status of the adult performers and the child audience. Sita Brahmachari (Hornbrook 1998: 22) writes interestingly about an immigrant child from Ghana, who thought she knew nothing about drama because she knew nothing about Western drama. In fact she had expert knowledge of performance conventions relating to her own culture. If inclusivity is to be addressed, not only in classroom management and curriculum planning, but also in performances for multicultural classes, the onus is even more strongly on the devising team to research into the cultural background of the target audience before deciding on a theme and performance style. Ideally, the devising team should also be multicultural.

Drama is used in a variety of ways by practitioners whose aim is to effect social or political change. Epskamp (1989) gives a number of instances of drama used to promote hygiene and healthy eating in the developing world: short propaganda pieces with titles like 'Breast Milk is Best', 'Children Need Additional Food' and 'Eat More Vegetables'. Orr (1978: 78), commenting on the use of drama for the promotion of political programmes, recounts occasions in Vietnam and Laos 'when puppet theatre was used both by the communists and by the US Information Agency in order to win over the rural population' (cited in Epskamp 1989: 131). Epskamp makes a distinction between projects that encourage 'endogenous' development, change from the inside, and those that are 'exogenous', project orientated, based on outside intervention. In contrast to the exogenous projects referred to above, Boal's work in Peru and elsewhere, though clearly political in purpose, starts from issues of concern to the community and employs dramatic structures, 'image' and 'forum' theatre, which empower the audience to enter the political arena and rehearse alternative responses or courses of action. 'Boal does not so much speak about revolutionary theatre, but of theatre as a rehearsal, a preparation, for societal reforms (Epskamp 1989: 53).

Practitioners have also engaged in theatrical exchange. This is formalised in International Theatre Festivals, when authentic work from different cultures is presented without adaptation to an intercultural audience. A more direct and interactive form of exchange occurs in what Eugenio Barba described, in the early 1970s, as Barter performance.

> ...in Barba's theatrical barter, the commodity of exchange is performance. In its simplest form, a Barter entails one group of people performing for another, and, rather than the second group paying money, it performs for the first group. A skit is exchanged for songs and dances, a display of acrobatics for a demonstration of training exercises, a poem for a monologue. (Watson, 1993)

Working with his theatre company, the Odin Teatret, Barba has mounted Barters in a variety of settings in Europe, Latin America and Asia. An important feature of this work is that there is no pre-established value placed on what was exchanged. Each contribution is equally valued. What is important is the act of barter itself.

Barba was also engaged, through his work with the International School of Theatre Anthropology (ISTA) with research into intercultural theatre practice. Working with drama practitioners from all over the world, he is seeking to define universal pre-expressive principles common to different traditions.

> ISTA has given me the opportunity to gather together masters of both Eastern and Western theatre, to compare the most disparate work methods and to reach down into a common technical substratum whether we are working in the theatre of the West or in the East...At this pre-expressive level, the principles are the same, even though they nurture the enormous expressive differences which exist between one tradition and another, one actor and another. (Barba, in Pavis 1996: 220)

Like Barba, Peter Brook has been absorbed not by the cultural specifics of particular cultures, that which is observable at a surface level, but by a belief that there is an irreducible common relationship between performance and audience that reaches across cultures, developed or primitive.

> Brook has been compelled to search for a universal theatre language to articulate a universal art which transcends limited nationalism in an attempt to reach the human essence. (Pavis 1986: 6)

This led Brook to experiments like *Orghast* in which the myth of Prometheus was presented in an 'invented' language derived from ancient languages by Ted Hughes; and his journey across Africa with *The Conference of the Birds*, in which a variety of improvised performances arising from preparatory work at the *Bouffes du Nord* in Paris were presented to communities with no conception of Western theatre and a very different performance tradition, and which were received in a variety of different ways, from puzzled silence to spontaneous if uncomprehending laughter.

> The real lessons of the performances of *Orghast* and *Conference* was the difference between a closed form of theatre and one that's trying to be open to everyone. It's the difference between rarefied, aesthetic traps of myths and Greek tragedy, of the High Seriousness that goes with ancient and new language, compared to the power and naivety of an image which might be as simple as a bird emerging from an ordinary cardboard box. For, in that apparently mundane action might exist such direct-

ness and force, that the spectator is suddenly involved in all levels of meaning. If Brook can discover it, the form which gives expression to his ideal theatre will encompass everything from our deepest sense of myth to the slapstick of circus. (Heilpbern 1977: 191)

In choosing *The Conference of the Birds*, a twelfth century Sufi poem by the Persian mystic Farid Ud-din Attar, Brook was hoping to tap into universal experience.

> *Conference* offered Brook the possibility of a theatre of transcultural myth. The production foregrounded the poem's archetypal narratives: the thematic elements of struggle and search; the thirst for a beyond, a 'something more'; the transcultural bird idiom as metaphor of humanity's inner aspiration, its desire to transcend itself in flight. (David Williams in Pavis 1996: 69-70)

In selecting source material for what is appropriately described as transcultural (transcending barriers) rather than intercultural performance, Brook was constantly looking for narratives with archetypal and therefore, supposedly universal significance. He was looking beyond the local, religious, historical, the culturally specific, to narratives that exist on more than one level. In speaking of *The Ik*, Colin Turnbull's 'study of the demise of a North Ugandan tribe', Brook tells us:

> The Ik survive at a cost - and so do we. For me it's the perfect metaphor, something which exists at two levels - real in the sense of life as we know it, and real in the deep sense of myth. (Peter Brook in Oakis, cited in Pavis 1996: 69)

How does the Azerbaijan project sit in relation to the intercultural performance activities described above? Ostensibly we were taking drama workshops and short pieces of devised theatre to another culture. But, in order that the experience should be relevant to and intelligible to our audiences, this involved a reaching out, a taking from the culture of familiar stories and archetypes to create hybrid forms standing somewhere between our experience and that of the young people we worked with. We were committed to taking out a piece of educational theatre, not to preach but not simply to entertain. If opportunities for 'barter' or cultural exchange arose, we would welcome them. We had no expertise in drama therapy but hoped that the experience we offered would at least provide a distraction from the monotony of life in the camps, and at best touch them affectively in the way that theatre sometimes can. For us the process involved both research and experimentation. We had to select from our resources to learn how to communicate across the linguistic and cultural divide. And finally there was the fascination of visiting and working in a foreign country, sharing the life in the camps and responding to the challenge of the task we were engaged in.

## Categories of the Culturally Familiar/Culturally Foreign

Marvin Carlson's elaboration of Michael Gissenwehrer's categories of the culturally familiar/culturally foreign in intercultural performance (Pavis 1996: 82) provides a useful framework for discussing the drama projects taken to Azerbaijan, both in terms of theatrical style and content and in relation to the themes or 'learning areas' implicit in them. The parameters he identifies are presented in relation to a 'source culture' and a target culture: 'at one extreme is the totally familiar tradition of regular performance' and at the other 'An entire performance from another culture [is] imported or recreated, with no attempt to accommodate it to the familiar'. The full range of categories is replicated in a simplified form below, with Azeri culture as the target and British culture as the source.

## Target Culture: Azeri

- The totally familiar tradition of regular performance.
- Foreign elements assimilated into the tradition and absorbed by it.
- Entire foreign structures assimilated into the tradition, e.g. Noh[1] plays by Yeats, the Ninagawa Macbeth.
- The foreign and the familiar create a new blend, e.g. Moliere's absorption of Italian commedia into his new style.
- The foreign becomes assimilated as a whole and becomes familiar, e.g. Italian opera in England.
- Foreign elements remain foreign, used within familiar structures, e.g. the Oriental dance sequences in David Hwang's *Madame Butterfly*.
- An entire performance from another culture [is] imported or re-created with no attempt to accommodate it to the familiar.

*Source Culture: British*

In taking work to Azerbaijan there was no way, with our background and experience, that we could replicate local cultural traditions; and in any case, it is unlikely that the children who grew up in the camps would have had any direct experience of theatrical performance, such as might be seen in the theatres in Baku. If we had simply been concerned with intercultural exchange, we might have taken out a representative piece of contemporary British theatre, but this would not have allowed us to follow the TIE model presented in the first section of this article, with its emphasis on research and consultation, and the identification of a theme relevant to the experience or needs of the target group. The category which the work most closely approximates to is the penultimate in the scheme, 'Foreign elements remain foreign, used within familiar structures'. The use of Azeri stories as a framework for play making in the two-week residencies, and the use of significant and familiar mythological symbols in the devised plays, provide some link with the target culture. The style of performance, heavily dependent on mime, visual effects and clowning techniques emanates from a European performance tradition.

It is instructive to apply the above scheme to the theme or 'learning area' of the TIE programmes. The categories (below) explore the relationship between attitudes and values formed by cultural modelling, in the source and target cultures and, without forcing the comparison, provide a framework for discussing what ideas are being exported and why. From the perspective of the recipient culture the range of possibilities might be presented as follows:

## Target Culture: Azeri

- Totally familiar attitudes/thematic content.

- Some source culture attitudes assimilated and absorbed by the target culture. The audience may recognise and endorse such attitudes but do not necessarily see them as foreign and are not challenged by them.

- The blending of foreign and familiar creates a disturbance but can still be accommodated within the existing value system.

- Foreign attitudes are perceived as such, and though they may be presented within a context of familiar or shared values, they suggest difference and are seen as expressions of alterity.

- A foreign value system is imported in its entirety without any attempt to accommodate it to the familiar.

*Source Culture: British*

There can be no doubt that, simply by agreeing to work in displaced persons' camps in Azerbaijan, particularly under the aegis of an Aid Agency, we were asserting culturally determined values. That we should consider it appropriate to take out a drama project reflects our belief in the efficacy of drama as stimulus, solace or simply entertainment for young people living in difficult conditions, with little hope of improvement in the immediate future. The educational models we were exporting were tried and tested in the British context, but clearly had to be adapted to the needs and special circumstances of the target groups, particularly since they had no previous experience of drama or theatre. Through research and consultation we attempted to build a bridge between our culture and theirs, by basing the work on stories and symbols familiar to them, and by trying to identify themes that were relevant to their situation and experience. Our perspective as adapters was inevitably conditioned by our own cultural modelling and, while sensitive to values and attitudes in the target culture which it would be inappropriate to challenge, there were occasions when, in order to fulfil the learning objectives, particularly of the TIE programmes, we presented attitudes that were closer to home. JanMahomed (1985), in an article on colonialist literature, identifies three possible relationships between the Self and the Other:

> Faced with an incomprehensible and multifaceted alterity, the European theoretically has the option of responding to the Other in terms of identity or difference. If he assumes that the he and the Other are essentially identical then he would tend to ignore the significant divergences and to judge the Other according to his own cultural values. If, on the other hand, he assumes that the Other is irremediably different, then he would have little incentive to adopt the viewpoint of that alterity: he would again turn to the security of his own cultural perspective. Genuine and thorough comprehension of Otherness is only possible if the self can somehow negate or at least severely bracket the values, assumptions, and ideology of his own culture. (JanMohamed 1985: 64)

Since Azeri culture, because of Russian influence and the secularisation of the society, appears more Eastern European than Middle Eastern, it has been possible to identify commonalities, though not to be unaware of 'significant divergences'. While I would agree that it is important to 'negate or at least severely bracket' one's own cultural values in order to gain an understanding of other people's, these can never be entirely switched off, and in some instances it is important that they should not. Attitudes to disability presented in one of the plays would be not be perceived as 'foreign' by the Azeri audience, but would endorse their own value system. On the other hand, actions that suggested an inversion of status in gender relationships would be received with a gasp of surprise and perceived as expressions of alterity.

It would not sit easily to reinforce target group attitudes which were clearly at odds with our own strongly held beliefs, or at the other end of the scale to use the drama as a vehicle for imported propaganda. However, in the middle ground between the culturally foreign and the culturally familiar lies the possibility of meaningful, thought-provoking and affective communication.

## The Target Audience

In Robertson's *Travellers' Tales: Narratives of home and displacement*, the voice of the exile is frequently heard. While part of the 'nightmare' is 'to be uprooted, to be without papers, stateless, alone, alienated and adrift in world of organised others' (Robertson 1994: 93), several refugees refer to their experience as existing in a limbo between memory of what was and uncertainty about the future. 'Like so many others, I am preoccupied by ideas of home, displacement, memory and loss' (Robertson 1994: 93). Bessie Head, an exile from South Africa, is described as 'having inhabited a twilight zone between fading memory and unrealisable expectation...All exiles, whether writers or not, share a certain churning of the stomach as they ride the emotional waves between memory and expectation' (Robertson 1994: 116). For the adults in the Azeri camps the memories of home and sense of loss is still keen. There is little hope that they will return to their homeland and very few have been relocated or found employment beyond the confines of the camp or its immediate locality. One of our interpreters, who had lived with her family for several years in the camps, had been able to complete her education and was now employed by the Leonard Cheshire foundation and living in Baku. But this was unusual. For most of the men there was little to do except try to scratch a living from the stony ground, provide an occasional taxi service for visitors, but more usually play dominoes and smoke for recreation. The women were busier, engaged in domestic tasks, hand washing the family's clothes, and cooking on primitive stoves in cramped conditions or out of doors. For the children there was school for half a day, and little to occupy them for the rest of the time. Any break in the monotonous routine, like the arrival of a food shipment, or visits by aid workers, brought out a crowd of men and children eager to observe or participate in the action. Many of the children could remember no other life, but their memories of their homeland were sustained by the stories told by their parents.

## Audience Response

While one of the challenges for us was to communicate across both cultural and linguistic barriers, both in the selection of activities for the workshops and the form and content of the plays, ultimately the readability of the work was dependent on the cultural and artistic filters applied by the mixed audience, whose individual responses would vary greatly, depending on age, preoccupation and experience and, in the absence of certainty about what they were watching, a tendency to read into the performance whatever would make sense of it, or what they wanted to see there.

> the foreign culture...is transformed in the memory of the spectators. At the end of the process, when spectators feel themselves buried alive under the sand of signs and symbols, they have no other salvation than to give up and turn the hourglass upside down. (Pavis 1996: 1)

While, in Pavis's analysis the spectator is motivated to make sense of the performance by relating it to his/her own cultural frame of reference, Bennett (1997) suggests another kind of response, particularly in cases where the cultural context of the performance is very far removed from the spectator's own life experience. Bennett reflects on her response to an Aborigine song and dance ritual, the 'Inma', which was so far beyond her cultural frame of reference that she felt that '[her] strategies of viewing were not only disabled but irrelevant' (Bennett 1997: 194). She engages in a willing suspension of her usual rational, analytical, intellectual stance, 'the abandonment of what one knows, the admission of what one does not know' in order make space for the emergence of 'skills in listening and seeing which refuse to move easily into received models of both production and reception' (Bennett 1997: 195).

Audience expectations translate into an expectation without expectations, a spectatorial gaze unmoored from its anchors of knowingness. The operation, then, becomes translation grounded by a willing failure to know. (Bennett 1997: 195)

Susan Melrose (1994) makes a similar point when she suggests that there is something vital to do with subjective, affective response missing from the 'nominalised' systems of Elam and Pavis. The Azeri audience, confronted with a performance that contains elements that are both familiar and foreign, will be engaged in the construction of 'new meanings'.

It is at this location of 'new meaning' that intercultural theatre holds out its promise, which includes, among other things' a liberatory potential for all its participants and perhaps especially the audience. (Bennett 1997: 196)

A subjective, affective response to the work lies as much in what the audience wishes to discover in the performance as in what was intended by the creators of the performance text.

## The Drama Projects

The BA Drama and Education Course at the Central School of Speech and Drama includes three units which allow students to apply their knowledge and experience of educational drama and theatre practice in selected educational settings. In 1998 two students piloted a two-week placement in a displaced persons' camp in Azerbaijan, funded by the Leonard Cheshire Centre for Conflict Recovery. This project, an Arts Residency, in which students work in one camp with a more or less fixed group of children, is now in its fourth year. In 1999, following successful TIE work with Bosnian refugees in an inner city London school, a second project, involving four students, was sent out to tour a devised TIE programme around several camps. This project was followed up by a second in the summer of 2000. In the case of the Arts residency, the student project is supervised by the Leonard Cheshire representative in Baku, and supported by local interpreters. The TIE project, which is degree classified work, is also seen during a brief visit by a supervising tutor from CSSD. In each case the work is essentially the students' own, and the tutor's function is to support, advise and eventually assess. The Leonard Cheshire Foundation is perceived as the host and helps the students to identify appropriate objectives within the brief already laid out in the unit outline.

## Consultancy and Research

The Leonard Cheshire staff and representatives have been very generous in giving time and materials to each student group to help them understand the context in which they will be working, and the role played by the Leonard Cheshire Centre in identifying medical needs and arranging visits by medical teams (see Leonard Cheshire website). The drama project is seen as complimentary to their main medical mission in that it takes a holistic view of the children's needs, and seeks to provide stimulus, enjoyment and opportunities for creativity. As each student group has returned, more information has become available, gathered through conversations with the interpreters, teachers, and students in the camps; from photographs, videos, and audiotapes of traditional and popular local music; from visits to the Baku puppet theatre; and through written reports and evaluation of the drama work. Further information has been gathered in this country through consultation with, for example, Zulfugar Ahmedzade, an Azeri poet working for the BBC World Service, who put us in touch with a specialist on folklore and mythology; from supplementary lectures by specialists involved in intracultural work; by attending and contributing to international conferences; and through library research and information drawn from the Internet. Last summer a group attended a concert at the Festival Hall, given by Alim Qasimov, the renowned singer of the Azeri mugam, which gave them insight into the passion, beauty and complexity of the mature culture.

In all of this, what has been impossible to achieve, because of the difficulty of communication with the camps, is advance contact with the Azeri teachers or camp leaders, to explain what we were doing, consult them about appropriate topics, and to attempt to set up both preparatory work before our arrival, and the possibility of follow up after our departure. On some occasions, after the performances, it was possible to speak to the teachers, to get valuable feedback on the work, and to talk about how it might develop. But these conversations were all too brief, and in general, particularly in relation to theme and content, our decisions were informed by intermediaries: the two accompanying interpreters and the Leonard Cheshire representatives who knew the camps well; and by accumulating information from the students involved in the projects.

## The Arts Residency

On each occasion the students stayed in Echo camp in Saatli, not far from the Iranian border, and travelled daily to a second camp some distance away. They worked with a large group, up to 80 children, though the numbers varied daily, for four to six hours a day. The activities included a variety of games and interaction activities, the dramatisation of a simple story made up by the children, derived from local folk tales, puppet and prop making, and at the end of the second week, a short performance. Each returning group has given a full account of their experience, and recommendations for the development of the work, to the group going out in the following year. The difficulty in maintaining continuity over the two-week period has led the group going out in April, 2001, to approach the work in a different way. Rather than work towards a semi-scripted and performed product at the end of the fortnight, they will work on a daily basis with whichever children choose or are able to attend. They will approach the work more as a series of relatively self contained drama lessons, possibly related to stories, or to relevant themes, and trying out a variety of approaches, mime, movement, talk through story, teacher in role, appropriate in this country at Key Stages 1 and 2. While in previous years, the students have had the help and support of two adult interpreters, one of whom is a qualified teacher who has taught in the camps, this time they will be joined by two students from the Baku Language University, who will share their accommodation in the base camp, and provide invaluable support in the daily work with the children. This is an important development and coincides with the withdrawal of the Leonard Cheshire Fast Track referral programme from Azerbaijan and the handing over of their medical referral and logistical role to the two interpreters who have had so much involvement with the organization since the programme started. We are also hopeful, that, having made the contact with Baku Language University, the drama projects will continue, whether or not CSSD students can participate.

## The TIE Programmes

### Bear Tracks

As I indicated earlier, the starting point for this work was a TIE project based in an inner city London school, in which there were a number of English as Additional Language (EAL) pupils, including a group of recent immigrants who were refugees from Bosnia. In this case the student group were able to contact and take advice from the class teacher and language support teacher and decided to take as their theme the difficulties experienced by children who had been cast out of their own country and had to come to terms with the strangeness of another. Research into the children's background revealed that the bear was an important mythological figure in Yugoslav folklore, so they developed a scenario in which an anthropomorphic dancing bear, badly treated by a cruel owner, escapes to England by ship, finds the noise and bustle of the London streets terrifying and is befriended by an English child who takes him home with her.

The group developed a pre-pack, which was sent into school before their arrival and they conducted a workshop with the children after the performance. The play was performed in English, but the main points of the storyline were made clear through mime, action and physical theatre techniques. The mute bear was a powerful central character with whom it was easy to empathise, particularly when he was being forced to dance by his cruel slave master, or confused and frightened by the London traffic. The strong emotional elements in the play were balanced by moments of joyful clowning, song and dance, and clever visual effects. All the characters, except the bear, carried a small brown wartime suitcase containing their props and minimal costumes, which made transformations quick and interesting to watch. The performance was very well received by the young audience, who in conversations afterwards indicated that they understood what was happening to the bear and were concerned about him. What emerged from this performance that was highly influential on the work in Azerbaijan was the effectiveness of metaphor in delivering a story on more than one level, the fact that animal characters were easily readable across linguistic and cultural divides, and that strong emotional moments generate a strong affective response in the audience.

### The Hawk

Two of the students involved in this project had spent two weeks in Azerbaijan in the previous year working on the arts residency project. Their observations, photographs and videos, as well as reported conversations with a variety of people in the camps provided a valuable starting point for the work. Additional consultancy meetings in London provided information about Azeri culture and approaches to intercultural work. After considerable debate it was decided that the theme to be addressed would be attitudes to the disabled. The students had observed a group of able bodied children who regularly jeered at a young disabled man living in the camp they were staying in. In the same camp there was a thirteen-year-old girl with a wasting genetic condition, who hid herself away from her peers, never leaving the room in the abandoned factory building that was her home. We were assured that in Azeri culture the disabled were usually treated with sympathy and respect and that what we were seeing was the exception rather than the rule. This was helpful in that the values represented in the play would not be perceived as 'foreign', exported and imposed by another culture, but would in fact reinforce existing attitudes.

In our discussions with Zulfugar Ahmedzade, the London-based Azeri poet, we discovered that the hawk was an important symbolic figure in Azeri mythology. He lived high in the mountains above the villages, circling overhead and keeping watch on the people below. The students had also become aware of the Azeri custom of tying rags to a tree in order to make a wish or send thoughts to relatives far away. During the arts residency, groups of boys had very much enjoyed kung fu classes conducted by one of the aid workers. Observation of the (sometimes comic) day-to-day happenings in the camp provided other ideas for the play, a simple scenario was developed:

A hawk emerges from an egg and learns to fly. An old woman chases a squawking chicken. A group of hunters appear (kung fu movements) and shoot the hawk, which falls to the ground wounded. The old woman and the chicken mock the fallen hawk. An artist upbraids them for their cruelty and encourages them to help him bind the hawk's wing. A huge storm blows up. The old woman and the chicken are protected by the hawk, who does battle against the elements.

In a pre-play workshop the students introduced the children to a range of mime and physical theatre conventions they would see in the play: they drew mountains in the air; they represented natural objects in group tableaux; and they took part in a kung fu march. The performance was mimed with occasional sound effects, fragments of English for emphasis, and the accompaniment of a flute. This was a travelling show on a very low budget, so all the props and costumes had to fold-down in order to fit into suitcases and be carried by hand. The hawk was played by the one male student in the group wearing fold down withy and paper wings, which were wider than his arm span when extended. The chicken wore a comic hat and tail feathers, the old woman a shawl, and the storm a heavy blue cloak and face paint. The play and workshops were performed in a number of different venues, some of which were out of doors on the barren rocky ground of the camps in baking heat. I quote from the report I wrote immediately after my return in June 1999:

> On the stony, drab, dusty plain in front of the school hut the colourful, energetic, sometimes comic story of the hawk unfolded. At intervals in the action a family of geese, two or three cows and a tractor passed by in the background. The children loved the moment when G. flew over them almost touching the front row with the trailing feathers of his hawk's wing. A gasp went up as he leapt on to I.'s bent back (a woman providing strong support) to reach higher into the sky, and when I., as the badly behaved, squawking hen, replete with beak and tail feathers, approached the audience to peck at them. They went quiet when the hawk was wounded and lay struggling on the ground, and although they may not have understood the few English words spoken by the artist, they could tell from H.'s body language that she was angry with the hen for teasing the fallen hawk. In the final swooping battle between the hawk and E. with her storm cloak and painted face, the children may not have been entirely sure what she represented, but could tell that the hawk was heroic and eventually triumphant. (Harris 1999: 22)

In the post-performance workshop the students first asked the children, through the interpreters, what they thought the play was about and, since Azeri stories often have morals, what they thought the message of the play was. One articulate boy gave a clear account of the story line and others added comments on particular moments in the play. They seemed less sure about the message. 'Always have a chicken with you' was one interesting suggestion. The children were each given a paper feather and a coloured pencil and asked to think of an experience they had had, which, like the hawks, had been very difficult to cope with. The messages, written in Azeri, were later translated for us by the interpreters.

> I found it very difficult when we had to leave home.
>
> I found it very difficult when our car broke down.
>
> I find it very difficult being a refugee.
>
> I have many problems but my friends help me.
>
> Like the bird I want to fly back to my homeland.

These messages were attached to the hawk's wings and he took flight on a long swooping path around the school hut with 60 excited Azeri children at his heels. The metaphor we had intended was read by the Azeri audience in a different way, one that was meaningful to them. 'We thought we had taken out a play about broken limbs but it turned out to be a play about broken lives. The hawk had become a phoenix, representing the Azeri people's heartfelt desire for the restoration of their homeland' (Harris 1999: 22). Later in the week an Azeri teacher said, 'The hawk is Azerbaijan and one day Azerbaijan will fly again', and Matthew Fleggson, the Leonard Cheshire representative in Baku added, 'I thought one of the project's most valuable roles was to give the children an opportunity to articulate desires and concerns that, though of prime importance, they might not otherwise mention, or be encouraged to discuss (such as the difficulty of leaving their homes). The comments of these children, written on the paper feathers of the hawk, are the most expressive account of the project's value'.

### The Pond

A second TIE project went to Azerbaijan in June 1999. Closely modelled on the first, it again tried to embed a metaphor at the heart of the play, and again used anthropomorphic characters. Because the student group was more informed about intercultural issues, considerable debate surrounded the educational purpose of the work and the choice of an appropriate theme. Again, the difficulty of communicating directly with teachers in the camps meant that we were having to rely on secondary sources of information. However, there was now an increasing body of people we could refer to, including a growing number of students who had worked in the camps on one project or another. But, as one student said, 'Nothing quite prepares you for what you are going to find in the camps'. The theme selected reflected early discussion with one of the Leonard Cheshire representatives at the inception of the project: the courage, determination and effort required to do anything in a situation of dependency and disempowerment. There were examples that we could see around us in the refugee community of people who were making that effort: men scratching away at the stony soil to prepare a bed for vegetables; teachers doing their best to provide an education for their pupils with minimal resources, and to keep alive the strong musical tradition by running a small rhythm band; and women striving to care for their children in harsh circumstances.

The play told the story of a frog who lost his pond and set out on a journey, supported by two good friends, to find a new one. The style of performance was, in this instance, strongly influenced by clowning techniques, and included sequences of comic business, song and dance routines and slapstick. The visual aspects of the production were particularly strong; beautifully designed, brightly coloured costumes reinforced the comic style and clearly represented the three animal characters. In discussions with the audiences after the performances and from their drawings, it was clear that the children had no difficulty in identifying the frog, dragonfly and turtle from what they were wearing, or in reading the relationships between the three characters. The flirtatious dragonfly formed a romantic attachment for the frog, and the slow moving, elderly turtle, who was always losing his glasses or his book, was clearly wise and gave helpful advice. An interesting feature of the performance was the inclusion of some Azeri words, and opportunities taken by the audience of supplying words in Azeri for the missing glasses and so on. The fourth character in the play was a wizard who, at the beginning of the devising process, was a reasonably benevolent character, but who developed, both in appearance and behaviour, into a truly frightening figure. It was this character that 'magicked' away the pond. This was an instance when a cultural construct from the source culture, familiar to us in pantomime, was both 'foreign' and disturbing to the Azeri audience. For the adults the association with war was all too clear. For the children, it may have awakened fearful memories which were difficult to deal with.

The students were keen to build on the previous group's work by providing opportunities for audience participation and to set up a structure in which the children determined the ending of the story. The children became participants in the frog's journey, creating objects for him to relate to as he travelled. This group participation was rehearsed in the pre-play workshop, with the children providing ideas - a car was one. Because of the numbers involved, the difficulty of communicating through the interpreters, and the time available, it was impossible to implement the idea of allowing the children to find an ending. The students provided a happy resolution with the friends helping the frog to dig a new pond.

In one camp, a difficult venue because the performance was presented in very hot weather in a huge open space in front of the communal building, an audience of over 100 children and men were extremely responsive throughout the performance, laughed and applauded frequently, and joined in the participation sequence with enthusiasm. In this large outdoor setting the wizard seemed less threatening than in the indoor venues. Nevertheless, in comments made by the children afterwards, it was clear that there had been a level of disturbance which needed attention.

> I liked the dragonfly very much. When the wizard came I was scared. I thought she would take us. Not just the dragonfly I loved - but frog and dragonfly played very nicely.

> I loved turtle, dragonfly and the vulture/big bird (interpreter unsure about the translation). Frog was looking for water. Dragonfly helped him. And with that they both looked for water. The big bird did not let him find water. In this performance I loved everything. I was happy they came here. They make us happy with this performance. But this big bird played her role well - at first I thought it was our enemy but then I thought she played her role well.

> The frog became friends with dragonfly. They came together in the end. I loved a lot frog and dragonfly. Frog was looking for water and dragonfly helped him. This made me very happy - that actors came here. I think it was great and everybody loved this performance. I want to say I loved it a lot. At the end - frog and dragonfly became friends and this part made me feel secure.

While the children were happy to have seen the play, and particularly enjoyed the clowning of the three animal characters and the playful courtship ritual between the frog and dragonfly, the intervention of the wizard and the shattering of the idyll was shocking and frightening and awakened memories too closely related to their experience of war and displacement. The metaphor was all too graphically clear. Just before we left the camp an older boy showed me a realistic and detailed drawing of a tank. Although the happy resolution of the play helped to restore a sense of security, and the second child was able to distance herself from her fear by commenting on the actor's performance, there was no opportunity, because of the short-term nature of the project, to talk through or channel the strong emotions that had been roused. It is significant that the drawings the children produced in the post-play workshop were almost exclusively of the three animal characters, not of the wizard.

## Parachuting in

The drama projects have provided the students with a powerful learning experience, not least because at every step of the way we have held the work up for scrutiny and asked 'not only what we are doing, but also how we are doing it'. A real problem in applying the British TIE model described by Jackson at the head of this article has been in setting up consultancy and communication networks with teachers in the camps in order precisely to avoid the 'one off' nature of the activity. In the two-week arts residency students have had the opportunity to work for a longer period with groups of children, but again, because of the communication lines, it has not been possible to involve local teachers in the work or to ensure regular attendance by a fixed group of children. Over the three years a bank of knowledge has been built up through contacts in Azerbaijan and London, and through information and materials brought back by the visiting students, and gradually more Azeri nationals are expressing interest in or being drawn into the work in the camps. As is not infrequently the case in intercultural work, the ideal has been subject to compromise and adaptation, and while the projects have usually been received with appreciation and enthusiasm by the teachers and other adults who saw them, given the nature of life in the camps, a drama performance takes second place to the arrival of a food shipment.

It has been extremely challenging for the students to select and adapt models of drama and TIE practice to these very particular circumstances. They have become increasingly aware of issues surrounding intercultural work, have debated them hotly during the devising process and reflected on them in their evaluations. The work in the arts residency has gradually developed from a project leading to the presentation of a performed piece to one in which a range of different themes and approaches are tried out on a daily basis. In the TIE projects students have tried to identify themes relevant to the children's experience, and to give them expression through constructs familiar to them. The use of narratives with an embedded metaphor, particularly when the central symbolic figure had local significance, added resonance to the simple scenarios and allowed for interpretation on more than one level. The animal characters were immediately recognisable to the child audiences and, despite probable differences in association, created an immediate and familiar link between performers and spectators. While the students were initially concerned whether they would be able to communicate across the cultural and linguistic divide, this aspect of the work was less problematic than anticipated, and generally the children had a good understanding of the narrative line of the plays, though they were sometimes less able to articulate what they thought the plays were about. The readability of the performances was enhanced by the use of representational costumes and props, (the hawk's wings, the turtle's shell) and, when there seemed to be any doubt, by referring to the object by its Azeri name. In the second of the two projects a number of Azeri words and phrases were introduced, including the croaking sound produced by the frog. The children were introduced to mime and physical theatre techniques in each of the pre-play workshops. They needed no help in interpreting and responding to the comic business in the first play or to the pratfalls and clowning routines in the second.

All three plays, including *Bear Tracks* in London, as well as providing entertainment, focus metaphorically on aspects of the children's experience as refugees. The central anthropomorphic character invites identification as he experiences fear, loss and restoration. The response of the children to the wizard in *The Pond* was concerning, especially because there were no structures in place (apart from the post-performance workshop) that would allow the students or other adults in the camps to talk through the emotions engendered at a later stage. The story of *The Hawk*, on the other hand, released an affective response and a level of identification that enabled the children to express their feelings in the messages written on the paper feathers on the hawk's wings.

For the children involved in the arts residency, and those who attended the TIE programmes, the drama provided a welcome break from the monotony of camp life, and an opportunity to engage in or respond to creative work. The fact that a group of foreign students has travelled to Azerbaijan and been prepared to work in the refugee camps has gradually drawn the attention of creative and educational agencies in Baku. The most positive things in terms of the continuation and development of the project have been the interest shown by members of the Baku Puppet Theatre Company, who speak of taking their own work into the camps; the firm intention of the interpreters to support further projects of a similar kind; and the involvement of local students from Baku Language University. A pebble has been dropped into a pool. We hope the ripples will continue to spread.

## Note

1. No or Noh: The stylised classic drama of Japan, developed in the 15th century or earlier, using music, chanting, elaborate costumes, and themes from religious stories or myths. (Collins English Dictionary).

## References

Bennett, S. (1997), *Theatre Audiences*, London and New York: Routledge.

Bharucha, R. (1996), *Theatre and the World.*

Belgrade TIE Company, Coventry (1976), *Rare Earth: A Programme about Pollution*, (ed. S. Wyatt and M. Steed), London: Methuen.

Bolton, G. (1984), *Drama as Education: An Argument for Placing Drama at the Centre of the Curriculum*, London: Longman.

Conceison, C. (1995), 'Translating Collaboration: *The Joy Luck Club* and Intercultural Theatre', *The Drama Review*, 39: 3 (Autumn), pp. 151-66.

Epskamp, Kees P. (1989), *Theatre in Search of Social Change: the relative significance of different theatrical approaches*, The Hague: Ceso.

Harris, V. (1999), 'Fallen Flight', Drama: *The Journal of National Drama*, 7: 1 (Winter).

Heilpbern, J. (1977), *Conference of the Birds*, London: Faber and Faber.

Jackson, T. (1993) (ed.), *Learning Through Theatre: new perspectives on theatre in education*, London: Routledge.

Hornbrook, D. (1989), *Education and Dramatic Art,* Oxford: The Falmer Press.

Hornbrook, D. (1998), *On the Subject of Drama*, London: Routledge.

JanMohamed, Abdul J. (1985),'The Economy of Manichean Allegory: The Function of Racial Difference in Colonialist Literature', *Critical Enquiry,* 12, (Autumn), University of Chicago.

Leeds Playhouse TIE Company (1984), *Raj*, London: Amber Lane Press.

Marranca, B. and Dasgupta, G. (1991), *Interculturalism and Performance*, New York: PAJ Publications.

Pavis, P. (1992), *Theatre at the Crossroads of Culture*, London an New York: Routledge.

Pavis, P. (1996) (ed.), *The Intercultural Performance Reader*, London and New York: Routledge.

Robertson G. (1994) (ed.), *Travellers' Tales: Narratives of Home and Displacement,* London and New York: Routledge.

Said, E. (1993), *Culture and Imperialism*, New York: Knopf.

Schechner, R. (1988), *Performance Theory*, London and New York: Routledge.

Van der Leeuw, C. (2000), *Azerbaijan: A Quest for Identity*, Richmond: Curzon Press.

Bharucha (1990).

Watson, I. *Towards a Third Theatre - Eugenio Barba and the Odin Teatret*, London and New York: Routledge. A chapter appears in Pavis, P. (1996) (ed.), *The Intercultural Performance Reader*, London and New York: Routledge.

Watson, I. 'Ways of Understanding the Culture: Re-examining the Performance Paradigm'.

# Bordering Utopia: Dissident Community Theatre in Sheffield

*John Salway*

## The Seeds of the Project

Sheffield Popular Arts was set up in January 1998 to promote dissident forms of community performance activity in Sheffield. Our first project was the *Bordering Utopia* community performance which ran from May 1998 until the eventual performance in March/April 2000.

We were stimulated to launch Sheffield Popular Arts and to plan the community performance we eventually produced by the upcoming millennium celebrations. What exactly did we have to celebrate? Our first instinct was to write a satire on the whole idea of 'millennium'. We wanted to confront the cultural and political implications of an event that seemed to offer a very partial and skewed view of human history. What seemed to be happening was a kind of collective amnesia about the hugely inequitable and oppressive forces being promoted by governments in the West under the superficially celebratory banner of 'globalisation'. While a relatively small number of entrepreneurs were opening up the global market so that goods and capital could flow freely across national borders, various local communities in different parts of the world were finding their ways of life threatened by the drive for new profits from as yet unexploited natural resources in the forests, deserts and mountain regions they had sustained for centuries.

We were all too conscious of the apparently historic defeat of socialist ideas in the rise of Thatcherism in the 1980s and the collapse of communism in the 1990s. It was widely assumed that the end of history had been witnessed with the final victory of capitalism over any other form of organisation of human economic activity. But from our perspective as socialists who 'refused to lie down and accept our historic defeat', we felt the need for a revaluation of socialist ideas and beliefs as they have been discovered and developed through history. But this revaluation would be done through the medium of the performance arts of song, storytelling, theatre, film and video.

The background to the setting up of Sheffield Popular Arts included the inauguration of the 'Raise your Banners' festival of political song in 1995; the eightieth anniversary of the death of political singer/songwriter Joe Hill in the USA.

The festival emerged out of the cultural activism of the Sheffield Socialist Choir, one of the choirs to develop out of the Street Music movement of the early 1980s in the UK. Street bands were an integral element of the antinuclear campaigns that opposed the siting of cruise missiles in the UK. The music they played was a complex mix of several different radical and oppositional traditions, including the political folk, blues and jazz of American protest from the 50s and 60s, the older workers' anthems and ballads of the nineteenth century and a growing repertoire of international music from sources like the Popular Unity movement in Chile and Anti-Apartheid in South Africa.

In our early meetings in 1998, we produced a number of key questions that seemed to crystallise what the major issues of our revaluation should be:

- What is our relationship to land and resources as we enter the twenty-first century?

- Can communities negotiate real change so that they can mobilize new skills and resources?

- How do these changes affect the way that natural and human resources are used?

- Which kinds of labour should be prioritized and rewarded?

- Which sorts of social ownership can minimize oppression and exploitation but maximize personal initiative and choice?

- Where should authority and power lie?

- How do personal relationships work in times of stress and anxiety?

- Which are the forces which constrain or liberate people in their desire to form their own relationships in the ways they want?

- What is a 'family'? What is a 'community'?

So, we wanted to consider how a 'community' works (or doesn't work) economically, politically, culturally and psychologically. We were conscious, I think, that a great deal of socialist theorising about just and equal societies has concentrated on the first two and ignored the third and fourth.

Our community performance project would be informed and impelled by a spirit of social and political enquiry. We would invite people in Sheffield who shared our concerns to join with us to research and imagine the kinds of communities that would be able to meet the needs of authentic social living in the twenty-first century.

We went on to shape a narrative that would focus the research and enquiry and provide a possible structure for the performance:

The play will tell the story of a fictional family in a Sheffield cityscape which is displaced from its home by economic hardship and social exclusion, as it experiences the problems of homelessness and exile. The real physical journey of the family will be paralleled by a metaphysical travelling into the past and future, as particular outlaw or utopian communities are encountered, images realised, and voices called up.

The images, voices and events from these times and places will be routed first of all through the perception and imagination of the children in the displaced family. Their first contact will be with children in the other communities. Ideas will be expressed through text, music, song and visual images. The precise 'reality' of the communication will always be in doubt; but they will become driving forces in the lives of family members.

The final act/scene of the play will plot out arrivals and new beginnings for the family which are equally full of doubt and possibility. It may be that, during the course of the play, individual members will leave to go on other journeys and new members will join so that the family at the end is significantly different from the family at the beginning.

Our objective was to build the whole process of research and enquiry into the very structure of our performance so that we could share at least something of our journey with the eventual audience.

## Developing the Project's Workshops

Gill Walker (as director) and I (as writer) collaborated closely at every stage of the project's development. We organized three series of workshops in 1998 to explore key ideas. We planned to use improvisation, discussion and debriefing and encourage personal testimony from participants; we felt we could generate some embryonic dramatic and musical material that might find its way into the performance.

### Mapping the Ground

We called the first series 'Mapping the Ground'. It was an intensive process of three workshops on the evening of 27 May and morning and afternoon of 28 May. We focused specifically on the theme of homelessness. In the first workshop, participants were invited to invent a homeless character and given opportunities to develop it through hot-seating and focused self-reflection. We set up the fictional location of Harrop House Hostel for the Homeless and Gill and I worked in role as warden and voluntary helper. The fictional time of three hours covering the opening of the hostel, serving of supper and finding of sleeping space before 'lights out' was then experienced as a 'living through' improvisation. We de-briefed this experience and followed it with a further 'living through' of breakfast the next day.

In the second workshop, we concentrated on the historical moment of spring 1649 when some dozen digger communities, inspired by the ideas of Gerard Winstanley, were set up on common and waste ground in various parts of England. The movement aimed, at a time when the outcome of the English Revolution hung in the balance, to occupy unproductive land and put it to productive use; give work and homes for landless labourers, de-mobbed parliamentary soldiers and poor families displaced by enclosures; and press the revolutionary Parliament to act on behalf of the poor in respect of land rights and the practical realization of the ideal of 'commonwealth'.

We discussed these ideas, introduced information about contemporary food production, technology, communications and customs and negotiated an improvised drama fiction based on a map of a fictitious community with workshop participants. This fiction charted the arrival of a group of the poor, their clearing of the ground on a wooded hillside and the holding of a meeting to decide how to cope with a threatened attack by local people, tenants and servants egged on by a local landowning parson. I worked in role as a travelling leveller preacher bringing fraternal greetings from well-wishers, other digger communities and revolutionary regiments in the New Model Army. Later the improvised action was crystallised into a number of linked theatre images presented in collage with dramatic monologues uttered by specific characters - all written by the people who developed these roles.

In the third workshop, Gill began by leading a discussion on revolutionary change, desires for a better life and the experience of political upheaval. One participant gave some personal testimony about her own family history. Her great grandfather, Solomon Koczinski, left his village in Rumania with his family in response to a pogrom. He walked with family members across Europe to the Dutch sea coast from where they took passage to England on a merchant ship. This story sparked off some improvisations focusing on that journey of exile from Rumania before the First World War. Actual family names were adopted by actor-participants and the informant briefed them about biographical details. Scenes improvised included one where Solomon was questioned by a customs officer at an English port (a process involving the 'translation' between the two by his eighteen-year-old daughter) about his reasons for travelling to Britain, his work, what money and goods he had. There was a flashback scene - the house was surrounded by a chanting anti-Jewish mob, the family loaded what they could onto a handcart and trudged out of their village.

A second fiction was negotiated set in Sheffield in 1997, involving a fictitious great granddaughter of Solomon's who was living alone in a room in the house of a friend. She was paying a very low rent, therefore able, despite quite a low income, to live a comfortable life. This character faced the predicament, in one crucial scene, where she had to leave her room because her friend was selling the house and moving to London with a new partner.

In the final phase of the afternoon participants collaborated to produce a dramatic synthesis of the three fictions developed during the day. The theatre image sequence and dramatic monologues were shaped into a collage of scenes and voices from the digger community, the Rumanian village and contemporary Sheffield, intercut to highlight parallel experiences and perspectives. Participants once again were encouraged to write their own scripts, which were edited and adapted by Gill and me.

### Utopia Today

The second series of workshops involved three 3-hour sessions held on successive Tuesday evenings. For the first workshop, we produced a city street map showing the fictitious 'Union Road Housing Co-operative'. A thumbnail sketch of its history was supplied together with role cards for twelve characters. Participants were asked to select one of the sketched out role cards or invent a character of their own and profile it on a blank card. Each person was then asked to explain in role why and when their character had joined the co-operative. We mapped out the whole space of the large hall we were using to represent different parts of the building: kitchen, dining room, crèche, social rooms and personal living space.

Participants were invited to enter their personal space in role and begin to occupy and define it through mime and monologue. The arrival of a woman and her teenage daughter precipitated a discussion about rules and regulations. There was a scene where the fourth anniversary of the co-op was celebrated. Further scenes explored problems with equipment and machinery. In the debriefing of this session, participants strongly expressed their feelings of frustration and dissatisfaction. It had been dominated by the minutiae of daily life; there had been no sense of vision; it had been over-verbalised.

In the light of these reactions, Gill and I decided to change tack for the next two workshops. We needed to get away from kitchen sink realism; we should aim for more ritual/fantastic/surreal forms of representation - in fact, something more utopian. For the second workshop, we focused on the body: on gesture, mime, simple dance and imagistic language. We deliberately avoided character and dramatic dialogue. An extended physical warm-up dovetailed into improvised movement in small groups. Participants were encouraged to use their bodies to express abstract ideas of utopia.

One group shaped a frozen image involving four of them representing a luxurious armchair into which the fifth member reclined. A second group looked like the ring of dancers from Cezanne's painting, developing a series of twisting, rotating, knotting and unknotting movements which expressed the flexibility of a group working in intimate collaboration. A third group took the idea of a group at a distance from each other staying in close contact through a secret language of gestures and non-verbal sounds.

Participants were asked to write in free form, using blank sheets of white unlined paper to express their ideas of utopia in concrete poems, shape poems or other forms. These pieces were fragmentary, impressionistic, composed of thoughts, voices and images triggered by the activity of physical improvisation. Once again, Gill negotiated this diverse material into a dramatic synthesis.

In the final workshop of this series, we discussed the idea of 'community'. This was aided by a group brainstorming activity in which participants sat round a table and passed round plain white sheets of paper with key words, such as 'Nature' and 'Industry', written on the bottom. People were asked to write single words or short phrases in response to the key words and what had already been written by others, linking words and phrases up in chains or developing new branches so that each sheet looked like a tree or plant. They were encouraged to decorate their words or phrases or shape them in significant ways.

In the discussion that followed, participants spoke about changes in our conception of what a 'community' is. The idea of a shared geographical area or locality still strongly suggests itself. But the development of urban lifestyles has meant the break-up of simple face-to-face relationships in neighbourhoods. People seek their social identity and solidarity more and more in communications across distances. 'Communities' can be exiled peoples who maintain contact across the globe, or people who share a particular political or religious commitment or leisure interest. Where there are face-to-face relations, questions of relative freedoms and responsibilities are easier to reconcile - it becomes much more difficult with the real social fragmentation that comes with the growth of cities and the destruction of traditional communities rooted in the soil.

### Utopia in the Past

The third series of workshops ran on successive Wednesday nights between 14 October and 2 December 1998. Between July and October, in close consultation with Gill, I produced a partial script draft based on what we had read and discussed. We studied several novels: William Morris' *News from Nowhere*; Charlotte Perkins Gilman's *Herland*; Marge Piercy's *Woman on the Edge of Time* and Ursula Le Guin's *The Dispossessed*. We also read a number of historical, philosophical and cultural theoretical works: Mary Bernieri's *Journey through Utopia*; W. H. G. Armytage's *Heavens Below*; A. L. Morton's *The English Utopia* and Krishan Kumar's *Utopianism* and *Utopia and Anti-Utopia in Modern Times*.

We decided to explore extracts of text from some of these novels suitably dramatised or reproduced in forms that would aid dramatisation. Our aims were:

• To introduce various utopian ideas, motifs and images in ways that could be explored dramatically;

• To experiment with dramatic form as part of our preparation for producing the script.

We were still not certain what the central narrative would be, but we were aware that we needed to interweave several different stories. We might use historical and fictional narratives together. The workshops would help us to see how they might work dramatically.

In the first workshop we looked at the folk-utopian idea of the 'Land of Cokaigne'. We reproduced a poem printed at the back of Morton's *The English Utopia*, a print of Brueghel's painting and the lyrics and melody of a song I had written. After an opening warm-up, I explained Morton's explanation of the idea as the 'Poor Man's Heaven'. Agricultural labourers were promised freedom from work - typically, wineskins poured themselves down the throats of supine peasants, fatted pigs already roasted squealed to be eaten and entire landscapes were made of sweetmeats. Given the relentless, slogging hours of field labour undergone, it was an understandable fantasy.

Gill then led participants in producing a piece of Image Theatre. This involved shaping two frozen images: the image of the actual, showing an experience of oppression; and the image of the ideal, where the oppression is removed. We then worked on a transitional mime to change the first into the second. We looked at some charcoal sketches by Jean Millet of peasants at work on the Plain of Chailly. These were used to trigger group physical work on the images. One group showed peasants digging up swedes from a frozen winter field without tools, using rough-edged stones. For the ideal image, one rolled backwards, mouth open, while the others cupped their hands to pour in streams of wine. The mime was done in slow motion; gradually the constricted postures of swede-digging turned into open relaxation. In the debriefing we discussed the way in which carnival can be seen as a brief moment of Cokaigne.

In the second workshop we returned to the English Revolution. Participants were invited to dramatise the actual digger community of St. George's Hill. We supplied some text written by Gerard Winstanley in a number of letters and pamphlets and brought in the song *Stand up, you Diggers all!* with a newly composed melody. Gill set up the structure for the improvisation. A group of poor, landless labourers, dispossessed peasants and demobbed soldiers arrived on St. George's Hill on 1 April 1649. Participants mimed clearing the soil and putting up rough huts. In a parallel improvisation, two local landowners discussed what to do about this threat to property, morality and social order.

Phases of improvised and part-scripted action developed. A travelling preacher arrived while the diggers were ploughing; there was a confrontation with local tenants and labourers; and a flashback to a scene on the road when a radical woman preacher spoke at a wayside pulpit. She argued for the active and equal share of women in the coming commonwealth. Passages from *Stand up, you Diggers all!* were integrated into the action after a vocal workshop. A presentation of polished improvised scenes intercut and fused by a linking narrative written in the workshop was then devised.

Further workshops focused on *News from Nowhere* and *Woman on the Edge of*

*Time*. Extracts had been turned into dialogue. Gill and I discussed and wrote briefing sheets outlining the culture and history of the utopian communities here to help participants to get a grip on the characters and situations shown. There was an initial discussion in which we drew attention to the typical features of utopian fictions; notably the device of dream journey, the guide figure to lead the visitor, the journey from the margins to the centre with a growth in insight, the visitor's recognition of the darkness of his/her own world and the reluctant return to the depressing reality of 'home'.

The key scene we worked on in *News from Nowhere* was extracted from the 'Obstinate Refusers' chapter. Gill organised a full-scale rehearsal where we moved chairs, tables, rostra blocks and portable screens to represent a building site just off the upper Thames where old houses were being renovated. Participants took on roles as William Guest; the visitor; his guides Dick Hammond, Clara and Walter Allen; Mistress Philippa the sculptor; her apprentice daughter and other workers on the site. As we worked on the scene, we added action and dialogue to point up the differences between William Guest and the Nowherians.

In workshop five, dialogue and action were further clarified and polished. We added a section which led into the scene involving William thinking aloud about the fine state of the woodland, the abundance of flora, and the intelligent coppicing. We worked in particular on a final frozen image of the moment when all the workers on site toast the health of William Guest and his guides. William is slightly isolated to symbolise his tragic status as traveller/observer in Nowhere. He is caught leaning yearningly towards the linked arms and raised glasses, looking upwards at that powerful sign of creative comradeship.

Debriefing these sessions, we recognised that with the notable exceptions of Mistress Philippa and Ellen, William's later guide, female characters tended to be one-dimensional, many described as 'pretty'. On the other hand, Morris did evoke a society of changed relationships and his writing suggested nascent psychological insights. He deals with a breakdown in the relationship between Dick and Clara (mirroring his own with Jane Birkin?) which has only recently been healed, and he writes about a killing apparently triggered by sexual jealousy. Where Morris is weak in rendering realistic technological detail, he is more convincing in his sketching of the texture of human relationships.

Exploring *Woman on the Edge of Time* in workshops six and seven, we began with a singing workshop on a song inspired by Piercy's novel. This offered particular possibilities for performance - a jazz/blues style of singing with vocal percussion. Participants explored solo passages on a foundation of choral sound. We discussed key differences between *News from Nowhere* and *Woman on the Edge of Time*. It was felt that Piercy's world is more fully realised than Morris'. Where he had been vague about technology, she is precise in what she imagines. Of course, she has the advantage of considerable advances in scientific and cultural understanding during the first six decades of the twentieth century. Her novel seems thoroughly informed by the detailed ethnographic study of a whole way of life where Morris' is suffused by an atmosphere of Godwin-like anarchy.

Language has changed; for example, the possessive pronoun 'per' has replaced 'his' and 'her'. This shows the cultural shift from gender differentiation to the sense of a dynamic continuum of sexual identity. Men and women share a 'motherhood' which is no longer tied to biological reproduction; sexual relationships are freed from the burden of childcare and can explore desire fully.

But we also recognised important common features. Each, rather than focusing on the machinery of political control and social administration, is more concerned with patterns of practical human relations. Both Morris and Piercy share a vision of a decentralised society where real power has shifted to the margins.

In workshop seven, we decided to look at the rites of death and birth as represented in Piercy's novel. In chapter eight, she ironically juxtaposes a death in Connie's mental hospital (an old woman who 'kicked off last night' and is being taken by a porter 'down to the meat department') with the death of Sappho, a 'great shaper of tales', in the utopian world of 2139 that Connie (a poor hispanic in her home world) visits through a psychic time-travelling link with a character called Luciente. In chapter twelve, Connie is an active participant in a birthing ceremony when she becomes a co-mother with two others of a child about to be born from the communal womb.

Participants divided into two working groups to rehearse these events. We read extracts from the chapters. For Sappho's dying, we focused on the moment when her daughter Aspen weeps on her chest. Sappho asks for her hair to be cut. How could this be visualised dramatically? Luciente was standing absolutely still, to the left of and behind Sappho, who was lying full length on a bench: a steady vertical balanced by a steady horizontal. Connie moved fitfully in and out of this space, not yet in synch with what she was watching. We 'cut' to the moment when White Oak and Jackrabbit carry Sappho to the water's edge so she can feel the pull of the receding tide. Only a slight movement was necessary; the grief was held in a calm action.

For the birthing ceremony, we acted out the ritual as described in the text. Barbarossa, the male midwife, delivers the child from the 'strange, contracting canal' into the arms of the three co-mothers - successively, a black woman, a white man and a Latin-American outworlder. We counterpointed the action with phrases from the song; a solo voice sang the chorus like a tape loop.

Debriefing, we discussed the social, cultural and economic issues raised by Piercy's novel. One participant felt the absence of gender identities was a tragic loss. Wouldn't this lead to a confusion about identity? A contrary view was expressed that these 'clear' identities can be felt as psychological traps. They are deeply rooted, it was suggested, in structures of oppression. Was it not 'natural' to have two parents; one male, one female? Were Piercy's utopians not engineering a kind of motherhood which actually denies satisfaction to both parties in a biological union? Others felt that these changes would lead in time to a wiser form of parenthood. Was the role of 'father' not lost? Others felt that what was positive and useful would be absorbed into the role of co-mother. In effect, both traditional roles of 'father' and 'mother' would be dialectically synthesised.

## Further Research and Development

### Towards a Complete Script

Nine months passed between the final workshop of the third series and the start of rehearsals proper. Gill and I maintained contact and spoke with certain members of the potential cast. From the experience of the workshops, we decided on particular dramatic elements that would be necessary. The first was the Chorus of the Dispossessed. We imagined this operating like a Greek tragic chorus, commenting on the action, interrogating characters and intervening in the drama. It would be a critical presence, provoking characters to think and act differently. But in another sense, it would be nothing like a Greek chorus. The characters would not be members of a settled community, sharing a common history and culture. They would meet on the road, in transit, travelling across history, rootless. They developed in the complete draft script as a group of shadowy figures, ghosting across history, taking a number of guises, haunting the main action without the ability to affect it at all.

The second crucial element was the main fiction itself. We needed to root this in the world of 1999/2000 or not very far into the future. It would trace the actions of a particular utopian community trying to put itself on the map, campaigning for real changes in contemporary society. Community members would be committed activists united by common goals and beliefs. The Chorus of the Dispossessed had grown organically out of workshop improvisations and dramatisations. There was some embryonic material to be used. This included work on the Diggers in 1649 and on the two utopian novels we had considered. But there was very little to work on about the contemporary community. Gill and I began to cast around for possible models.

We came across the story of the remarkable 'Gaviotas' community of scientists and alternative technologists who re-planted tropical forest in a semi-desert region of Colombia, and improvised a series of ingenious practical solutions to problems of housing, energy production and supply, water conservation, recycling of waste and the production of food, while trying to steer a diplomatic course between local FARC units and 'security guards' employed by logging and mining companies. We spoke to activists in a number of existing communities in the UK, including two in Sheffield. We had contact with Laurieston Hall in Dumfries & Galloway where one of the steering committee visited to discuss a range of issues like how they were managing the woodland areas on the community estate.

While this research work was progressing, I began to put together a scene structure; the first structure was finished by February 1999. I used the Gaviotas experience to rough out a storyline in which a community of scientific activists were struggling to keep their community going in the face of extreme threats of military violence. I set the narrative some way into the future, imagining a time when a multinational company called IBP (International Biological Products) had developed their global corporate power to such a degree that they were running their own military forces. The community finds itself invaded and its activists have to escape over a mountain range to safety with IBP searching for them. I eventually rejected this because I felt it was an examination of dystopia rather than utopia.

The one I invented for the first draft script was also wholly fictional and also set in the future. It was called the 'New Harmony Living Technology co-operative'. I set the action in 2025 in the Amber Valley, Westlandia. Like the 'Gaviotas' community, 'New Harmony' is trying to pioneer scientifically advanced solutions to various problems of sustainable food and energy production and distribution. Like the Diggers in 1649, it arouses the suspicion and hostility of certain local inhabitants. The community is small, there are nine members, so it really operates like a large family, although it is clear that they intend to expand their numbers. Direct democratic decision making offers no practical problems. Membership of the community is by explicit invitation, so in that sense, it could be seen as elitist.

At the core of 'New Harmony' are Sandra Bernstein, her current partner and colleague, Hugh McGovern and her two daughters Rachel and Rosie. It becomes evident that the whole venture is the brainchild of Sandra and Hugh, a character who doesn't appear in the action until the second half. Not only are they working to develop new forms of foodstuff which can survive in near desert conditions but they are actively campaigning in the media and on the internet against international commercial conglomerate - Interrnational Biological Products. IBP has a reputation of using child labour in the Third World and of being particularly exploitative of its workforce and especially hostile to trade unions. The firm is involved in a cartel which is attempting to pilot through a huge dam project in a country called Aridia. The plan, as reported by Selena Joseph, a militant in the local campaign against this project, is 'to corner a sizeable chunk of irrigated land for some unregulated and very covert experimental projects...to use the terrain as one huge experimental laboratory...people who are actually living there will be white rats whether they like it or not.' 'New Harmony' community members, suffering a series of violent attacks on the grounds and property of their site, are suspicious that these were being deliberately sponsored or fomented by IBP.

A key dramatic device of this script was that Sandra Bernstein was writing a utopian novel. In the opening scene, Sandra is discovered at work, consulting notes on her study desk, beginning to write. As she writes, her thoughts are projected into dramatic action. The Chorus of the Dispossessed, six characters in search of a just community and an equitable way of life, appear almost as vehicles for her thoughts about key historical and fictional communities. As the 'New Harmony' community struggles to come to terms with threats to its existence and makes contact with campaigns round the world, so Sandra struggles to make sense of the utopian tradition of critical social and political thought which has given them energy and direction.

The real dramatic tension is centered on the kidnapping of Hugh McGovern by the guerilla campaigners in Aridia who are trying to spotlight the IBP dam plan in the arena of international publicity. Hugh becomes a willing captive when he realizes who has caught him, but he is unable to contact Sandra from his prison high in the mountains until he is visited by an embassy official. The letter arrives in the second half of the action; at the end, Hugh is released and reunited with his family and colleagues. The actual outcome of the campaign against IBP is left uncertain, but the future of the community seems secure.

This script was long - it would have taken well over three hours to perform. But we were contemplating a performance time of two hours maximum. Significant cuts would have to be made. I wrote it during July and August 1999 and we invited workshop participants and other activists and interested parties from the Sheffield Socialist Choir, Norton College and other participating community groups to a trial reading in September. It was suggested that there was a problem with the location of the whole action of the play in the realm either of history or a fictional future in a fictional geography. Would this help us give a convincing account of utopian communities and the social and political forces at work? Would the audience be able to grasp and understand so many references to other times and places in the action of the Chorus of the Dispossessed? Could all these narratives be made to cohere?

## Re-making the Play in the Rehearsal Process

But as the rehearsal process got underway in October 1999, a much more fundamental issue than these came to the fore. So far as the script for the scenes involving the Chorus of the Dispossessed was concerned, we were able to work with the substance of what I had written. Because I was able to use actual material generated by workshop sessions, the company members cast as the Chorus were able to identify quite closely with the action and dialogue. Of course, there were significant changes: new names for some of the characters were negotiated, there were amendments to the script, it was substantially shortened in particular scenes. In essence, though, what I had written in August 1999 was what we performed in March 2000.

This was certainly not the case with the script for the main action. Although the 'New Harmony' community had emerged in a general sense from the ideas, explorations and improvisations of the workshops, the characters and action were wholly my creation. Our attempt to improvise the 'Union Road' community had been abandoned after one workshop only, and none of this had found its way into the script. There were also some significant changes in the membership of the community company from participation in the workshop. A number of men and two women had dropped out and some new members had arrived. The Chorus of the Dispossessed, on the other hand, was constituted of actors all of whom had been involved from the very beginning of the project. The upshot of this was quickly apparent. We would have to remake the central fiction of the play in the rehearsal process itself. It was important that community company members, some of whom were not confident about their ability to perform, should be involved in the creation of the characters they were going to portray. This, after all, is a central strategy of community theatre practice.

Rather than being individually authored by me, the play had to be collectively authored by the whole company. As the rehearsal process developed, individual performers began to shape characters for themselves within the context of particular improvisation structures. The script was made dialogically. If individual actors were unhappy with a specific speech, they could rewrite it and try it in rehearsal. A typical pattern of composition was: the discussion of a scene by those involved in it; the improvisation of action and dialogue based on that discussion - which was either tape-recorded and later transcribed or written down in note form during the improvisation and later polished up; the write-up brought to a later rehearsal, read, discussed, argued about and amended by consensus. This process could generate a great deal of passionate involvement by all actors in what their characters *could* say. As writer, I did not always feel that this process lead to the most coherent dialogue and sometimes actors were bent on simplifying their characters and making them fit completely a particular ideological view about how they *ought* to behave. On more than one occasion, I was telephoned by particular actors to lobby me to include a specific word or idea in the refined re-write of their character's dialogue. Re-drafting rehearsals sometimes took on the feel of conference compositing meetings as the meanings of individual words were minutely analysed and alternatives proposed. But this was all a necessary part of the collective authorship of the performance.

As project writer I frequently found this a difficult experience. After all, I had laboured long over the construction of scene structures and the writing of the complete first draft itself. I felt it to be my baby. And now, here it was getting torn limb from limb with (I felt) scant respect for the aesthetic integrity and verbal economy of the characters I had drawn and the dialogue I had written. Where were the interests and concerns of the writer being looked after here? I found myself wanting to promulgate my rights as the individual author. But, of course, this would have been directly contradictory to the 'rights' of the community participants to shape a theatre fiction which truly expressed their own developing ideas and commitments. These were expressed through the medium especially of the individual characters they brought to birth and then developed, making and re-making them in the light of further reflection and under pressure of improvisation as they faced critical incidents in the life of the utopian community. Here is clarified for us the fundamental self-educative purpose of community theatre. The whole creative process, from first workshop to final performance, must be informed by that heuristic principle.

At first, we used the idea of the fictional conglomerate IBP to trigger scenarios for improvisation. In one such session, for instance, it was discovered that IBP were planning to acquire a tract of land immediately adjacent to the community's own site. We improvised the reactions of community members to this, including the planning of a local campaign of resistance and plans to target UK executives with e-mails. But the difficulty was that we were having to invent and elaborate a whole culture and history of activities before we could begin to improvise credibly. It was increasingly felt that we needed a concrete contemporary campaign to provide a real context for the building of the drama fiction.

It was about this time that we discovered the local campaign in Sheffield against the building of a supermarket and car park complex on the 'Tyzack' site in the south west of the city. This site was a long-derelict tract of waste ground that had become well known as a source of rare wild flower and insect life. It had once housed a steel mill, but the buildings had been long demolished. The local campaign that opposed the supermarket development had put forward a number of alternative proposals for how the site could be used, but their real argument was that there should be a process of direct consultation with local residents and other small business users. This ought to involve an open debate where local groups could put forward *their* plans for the site's use.

At about this time, too, the activities of the US retail giant Walmart were attracting attention from the national media, ethical consumers and anti-globalisation campaigners. It was rumoured that the firm was looking to acquire a chain of supermarkets in the UK to get a retail foothold over here. Evidence was being gathered by anti-Walmart campaigners in the US that they were using Third World suppliers for some of their clothing and electrical goods and were not too concerned to look into the unscrupulous treatment of workers, starvation wages, the use of child labour and the like. This was what enabled them to discount their prices and still make healthy profits. Out of our discussions round these issues emerged the fictional supermarket giant 'Floormart' and we had the beginnings of our real contemporary context.

Developing characters became a task not only for the regular rehearsal process (every Wednesday night beginning from 6 October 1999) but also for informal meetings between individuals and small groups. For example, the two women actors who took on perhaps the two central roles in the performance met to decide together how *their* characters would relate. Sheila decided to take on the character of Sandra Bernstein much as it had been written in the August draft but with some significant modifications. Sandra would be writing a book about utopian communities but it would be an academic study rather than a novel. She would *not* be an activist in the community, but her daughter Rachel would be. Sally, a student from Norton College, took on the role of Rachel - attracted by a character who was her own age and facing similar life choices. As they worked together on the relationship between mother and daughter here, it transpired that Rachel's activism and decision to join the community would be a trigger for tension and conflict between them. Sandra's attitude towards the community would be ambivalent; she would regard it as a distraction from Rachel's proper path through A levels to university, although objectively seeing the protest as a good thing.

The other woman actor, Heather, developed a character eventually called Carol Godwin. She had a crucial scene with Sandra when she told her about her daughter's skills and flair for community campaigning, which would be a turning point in Sandra's attitude towards the community and Rachel's participation in it. Heather developed Carol Godwin as quite an experienced grass roots' political activist; she had, for instance, been involved in the setting up of the Greenham Common Women's Peace Camp as a young woman herself. The skills of non-violent direct action she developed became useful later on in the life of the community, 'Burncliffe Eco-Protest' as we later called it.

The first scene in *Bordering Utopia* is set on the site of Burncliffe Eco-Protest some months after the occupation has ended. In this scene, Sandra Bernstein and Carol Godwin rummage through the remains of the protest community, finding items that trigger off memories of the time of occupation. The two of them see a defeat but also developments from it. The action then flashes back to the first day of the occupation and actors enter in role as community activists to put what has been broken and scattered back together. This second scene was clarified for us when we chanced on a particular campaigning website called 'The Land Is Ours' - a site whose title page included a quotation from Gerard Winstanley.

'The Land Is Ours' collective, which includes the environmental campaigner George Monbiot, was responsible for a protest occupation in the spring of 1996 at a site in Wandsworth, south-east London owned by Guinness, the food and drink multinational based in Ireland. We came across a media record, including a number of newspaper articles and some correspondence about the 'Pure Genius' (an ironic reference, of course, to an advertising slogan of the time used by Guinness) campaign leading to the occupation of the Wandsworth site which, like the Tyzack site in Sheffield, was a tract of urban wasteland. The 1996 'Pure Genius' protest was planned as a short-term occupation of the Wandsworth site by a group of dedicated environmentalist activists. The occupation was highly organized, at least in the early stages. A number of experimental living structures were introduced on to the site, involving the ingenious use of cheap or recycled materials. Occupiers planted trees, shrubs and flowers and tried to design interesting pathways and decorate walls; artistic self-expression was enthusiastically encouraged. The idea was to show how, with imagination and the minimum of material resources, it was possible to develop sustainable, locally controlled structures which would meet the critical need for long-term affordable living and recreational space, rather than obey the dictates of the global economy, with its predatory, short-term impact on the local communities who believe they are inviting long-term solutions to their economic problems.

The action of the second scene of *Bordering Utopia*, therefore, reproduces the sense of energy and urgency on the opening day of the occupation which comes across in a short film about 'Pure Genius' we were able to acquire from 'The Land Is Ours' at its Oxford base. We mirrored the meticulous planning done by the occupiers to manage day-to-day material needs like food, the recycling of waste, the harnessing of wind power, the construction of semi-permanent living structures and the design of communal play and leisure space. In our action, we showed the occupiers of Burncliffe Eco-Protest quickly realizing they must gain the support of local residents and traders if they are to establish a secure foothold on the site. They must provide attractive but safe playing space for local children and contact local people to identify what they can do to help them.

One of the community company members who became involved some way into the final workshop/rehearsal process developed a particularly significant new role. This was Mrs Harris, an elderly local resident (inhabiting one of the flats in the block overlooking the occupation site) who was the first person to respond to the occupation. She was hostile, threatening to call the police, shouting out that what they were doing was illegal. Linda, the company member, began to map out a personal history for her which gave an interesting concrete historical dimension to the Burncliffe local community. Mrs Harris had lived there since just after the Second World War. She remembered the Labour government that was elected in 1945 and the huge wave of popular enthusiasm that greeted its accession to power. She recalled the building of the flats that was part of the local programme of slum clearance; she spoke of the river as being a place of real beauty - with kingfishers hunting in the clear water. Her husband, now dead, had been a keen fisherman. She was the last one of her generation still to be living in the flats.

Half way through the rehearsal process, we began to rethink the Third World connection that had been so vital to the August draft. We wanted to keep this international dimension in the action in order to show the global reach of Floormart's activities. A subplot should be developed which focused on a particular Third World economy; perhaps a contact could be made on the internet by one of the Burncliffe activists with an activist campaigning against the activities of Floomart in the country in question.

I discussed this in particular with some members of the Zimbabwean vocal and dance troupe Sunduza who were in Sheffield at the time. We were able to construct a character called Simon Moyo who became the Third World connection in *Bordering Utopia*. It was explained to me that, in common with many African economies, Zimbabwe's pattern of food production had been substantially distorted by global pressures to meet demand for foodstuffs from Europe and the USA. Production of food for home consumption now largely took place on marginally productive land where yields per acre were low; on the most productive land, cash crops for Europe were increasingly being grown. The upshot of this was that it was getting more difficult for Zimbabwe to feed its own people. Sally developed her character Rachel Bernstein to be the Burncliffe internet contact with Simon Moyo; surfing the net to find other global activists against Floormart, she came across his campaigning website.

### Constructing the Performance

We performed *Bordering Utopia* at the English Literature Theatre Workshop of Sheffield University on 29 March-1 April 2000. The ELTW is used as a teaching space for students doing English and Drama degrees at the University and for some Adult Education courses. Bill McDonnell, recently appointed as the Community Liaison Tutor, part of whose brief was to develop the space for local community use, invited us to be the inaugural project.

The performing space itself is very small with accommodation for an audience of only 75. There is a small entrance hall, minimal backstage space, no wings, but a gallery running round three sides of the black box that constitutes the whole space, leaving the cyclorama wall clear. Given the complexity of our performance. It was going to be difficult to fit the show into the space we had.

We needed to represent the occupation site itself, Sandra Bernstein's house (or *part* of it), the local flats where Mrs Harris lived, the space where Simon Moyo interfaced with Rachel Bernstein and have an undefined area where the Chorus of the Dispossessed arrived on their journey through various historical events. We also needed to provide space for our small band of live musicians and trio of singers, who would be contributing five songs and various pieces of instrumental accompaniment to the dramatic action. A composite set would have to be designed with at least some naturalistic detail of the occupation; it would also have to be flexible enough to be easily dismantled so that it would appear to be smashed for the eviction scene and then quickly put back together again for the following performance. We would have a screen on the cyclorama wall where sequences of film could be projected.

A professional designer was brought into the picture. As part of the process of design, community company members who had a particular interest in the materials to be used and ways of constructing them got involved in research. Visits were made to a number of alternative communities in the UK such as Tinker's Bubble and to 'The Land Is Ours' base in Oxford. Attention was given to which structures would need to be realistically represented and which would be practically used as part of the dramatic action.

Given the limited space available, we considered the possibility of creating a total environment for the performance so that the audience, as soon as they entered the front door of the building, would have the impression of being inside the occupation site of a protest community. We looked at the possibility of a large canopy slung from the roof above the lighting rig so that the auditorium would feel like the communal meeting space inside the occupation. But, for a range of safety reasons, we concluded that this was impractical.

The final design placed a 'bender' structure and a small windmill UR, with a planted terraced area in front and a platform set up for the musicians and trio of singers. UL was an easily-collapsible multi-purpose table with a rack overhead hung with cooking and cleaning implements. There was just enough space between bender and table for actors to enter UL. DC was left relatively undefined; but DL, built up on a rostrum block set against the wall, was a section of Sandra Bernstein's study including chair, table and portable computer equipment.

The computer was linked up to the screen so that Sandra's typed drafting of her book could appear immediately projected there for the audience to see. Key pieces of text triggered off the action of the Chorus of the Dispossessed. Simon Moyo also appeared on screen in his office in Harare as Rachel logged on to his website on the net. At various points in the performance, footage from a number of different occupations and protest actions was cut into the live action; this included sequences from Kevin Brownlow's *Winstanley* to counterpoint the scene involving the Chorus of the Dispossessed in role as Diggers.

We used the Tyzack site itself to shoot the scene when the Chorus of the Dispossessed first enter the action. This is a long shot which is held as the Chorus walk towards the camera across the wasteland. The Chorus then actually enter live into the performing space the moment after they walk out of the frame on the film, arriving on the site of the Burncliffe Eco-Protest itself, evidently having travelled far.

## The Community in Question - Connections and Commitments

The process of managing the project was taken on by a steering committee comprising Gill and me as joint project managers, Kaz Sludden, Dug Orton and Jane Thomas. The management of the project included the legal constitution of Sheffield Popular Arts itself, applications for project funding and financial oversight, monitoring of community involvement and strategic decisions about the overall direction of the project.

Sheffield Popular Arts has its roots in what might be called a dissident arts sub-culture in the city. I have referred earlier to the short history of the 'Raise Your Banners' festival of political song, organised and developed by activists in the Sheffield Socialist Choir. A theatre company called Rebels United was set up in 1995 as part of the inaugural festival specifically to perform John Fay's play *The Dream of Joe Hill*. Certain members of this group went on to perform a programme of short plays by Michelene Wandor and Caryl Churchill's *Vinegar Tom* on separate occasions. A planned production of Howard Brenton's *Greenland* - itself a notable dramatic treatment of some of the utopian themes and ideas explored in *Bordering Utopia* - was abandoned when there was a dispute between cast and director.

A significant number of members of the Rebels United Company became involved in the *Bordering Utopia* workshops and eventually in the community company, providing a core of committed participants. The project workshops and the final rehearsal process were publicised via various arts and community networks throughout the city but especially amongst performing arts students at Norton College, WEA students on the evening course 'Songs of Struggle' (which has generated Sheffield Socialist Choir), musicians in the fringe and community groups 'Ragnarok' and 'Lemon Soul' and activists in certain grass roots green and anti-globalisation organisations working in Sheffield.

I have made some references 'on the hoof', in my description of the way the project developed in practice, to certain principles and processes of community theatre. But can the project truly claim to be a piece of community theatre? After all, it was engendered and led by a small group of committed activists who, although living in the city of Sheffield, shared no common residence in a particular neighbourhood. We did not address ourselves to the needs or perspectives of any identifiable social or ethnic group.

The city, as a matter of fact, has a considerable history of community theatre in this pure sense. Sheffield Popular Theatre, for instance, was operating in the 1980s on the Manor, a working-class council estate. Its work was rooted in the particular culture and social experience of people living on the Manor, many of whom worked in the steel industry and its ancillary trades. This reminds us of the historical roots of the community theatre movement in the cultural effort of the 1950s and 60s to give voice to local working-class experience in history and in the contemporary world. Much artistic and media activity just after the Second World War appeared to ignore the concrete daily experience and perspectives of most of the population. It was still rooted in a culture dominated by middle-class and south eastern concerns and ideas. In film, TV, the novel, poetry and drama, as the fifties and sixties developed, working-class and regional voices began to speak, write and project images of this hidden or misrepresented experience. Community theatre can now be seen as one source of this burgeoning cultural energy which revolutionised the post-War world and began the pressure to demoticise and democratise every aspect of social and economic life.

But *Bordering Utopia* has developed in a very different epoch. It was still possible to think about the construction of a truly common popular culture in the immediate post-War years, although there were certainly passionate arguments about what ought to constitute it. At the end of the nineties, we look out on a cultural landscape that has shifted seismically. Other radical voices have spoken; notably those of women who have challenged versions of popular culture and history which ignore their specific experience of discrimination and oppression. Established ideas about what constitutes a 'national' culture, already being challenged by voices from the regions and from Scotland, Ireland and Wales, were even more radically contested by film-makers, novelists, poets and dramatists who spoke of the experience of ethnicity from a bewildering range of perspectives.

Our 'community' is very much a community of this culturally fractured era, living in a city which has itself experienced another industrial revolution that has dislocated any number of local communities who relied on the steel trades for a measure of prosperity. The question of how communities are to regenerate, rediscover confidence in their own resources and creativity, rebuild housing, services and local employment that can actually be sustained for more than a few months or years, is a burning one in Sheffield, as in many cities and towns of the midlands and north.

Community artists have perhaps always been bricoleurs. They have had to work with whatever they could pick up wherever they were, understanding the difficulties of people who come along, unsure of their commitment, uncertain of their skills, but wanting an outlet for a creativity that has struggled its way at least into partial light. Our experience on the *Bordering Utopia* project was of a shifting population, some of whom came perhaps only to one or two workshops and then disappeared, some of whom left because they were not happy with the political beliefs that underpinned what we were doing, some of whom joined very late and brought unsettling but important new ideas and perspectives. But there was always the core of committed participants who were going to stick with it through thick and thin.

We were, then, a particular community of interest and concern who held the dramatic mirror up to the nature of 'community' itself. What we produced was no earth-shaking blueprint for a just society; but a theatrical record of a particular journey of the imagination which tried to engage with important real landmarks in utopian socialist and feminist thinking. In this journey, I'd like to argue, the four performances were not the ultimate destination but simply important way stations. In the practice of community theatre, it is the journey itself which is the destination. There was inevitably much discussion and creative production all the way through the workshop and rehearsal process which did not find its way into the artistic statements of the performances themselves. I have presented only a very partial and fragmentary narrative of the many travellings in and out within the journey that were made by participants. Perhaps a number of participants did only come to one or two workshops. But who is to judge the quality of their experience and what they personally discovered about theatre and drama in those relatively brief encounters?

Krishan Kumar has suggested that at the close of the twentieth century, there is no longer any room for utopian manoeuvre; the tragic experience of the last 100 years has been the kiss of death for utopian thinking of any kind. But, in the middle of a world in which new oppressions, injustices and inequalities are being fomented and even institutionalised, the critical and satirical energies of a utopian tradition which highlights the darknesses of contemporary reality as it sketches the brightness of human possibility seems to me not just useful but necessary.

Why should community *theatre* still be so important a cultural and artistic practice? Are we not living in an era when theatre has been marginalised and rendered irrelevant as a form of popular expression? Hasn't it been cast into the dustbin of cultural history by the growth of electronic media and information technology?

If we are looking at the potential of new forms of communication and their impact on live performance, theatre has shown itself to be admirably flexible and imaginative in the way in which it has appropriated and integrated them into performance texts. We tried to do what we could on a very limited budget in our performances of *Bordering Utopia*. Under the pressure of new techniques and technologies, there has been a real expansion of the scope of dramatic form in live performance. Theatre remains in important ways the confluence of all the arts and media.

Its greatest strength remains, of course, the fact that it is the art form which is the closest to the textures of actual social life. Although capable of exploiting the potential of complex technologies, in essence it requires simply the presence of human beings together in a shared time and space. To make it requires only the ability to move and speak. It is truly accessible to everybody, if only they can overcome the barriers that stop them believing in themselves.

# Index